GBBS Pro

BULLETIN BOARD SYSTEM

Version 2.2

Produced by:
Brian Wiser & Bill Martens

 Apple PugetSound Program Library Exchange

GBBS Pro Bulletin Board System: *Version 2.2*

1s printing: July 2017. 2nd printing: June 2019. 3rd printing: February 2023.

Paperback ISBN: 978-1-387-00167-5
Hardback ISBN: 978-1-387-00169-9

ACKNOWLEDGEMENTS

GBBS manuals published 1980-1990 and *GBBS Pro*, *ACOS*, *ExFer*, and *SuperTAC* software
Copyright © 2017 by Kevin M. Smallwood under the GPL v3 License:
https://www.gnu.org/licenses/gpl-3.0.en.html

This new and expanded *GBBS Pro Bulletin Board System: Version 2.2* book is a copyrighted
production of Apple Pugetsound Program Library Exchange (A.P.P.L.E.) and has been
produced with permission of and in coordination with Kevin M. Smallwood.

GBBS Pro software and resources are on the official site: https://gbbs.applearchives.com.
No warranty of these items is made or implied and should be used at your own risk.

Special thanks to Lane Roathe and Paul H. Lee for the enormous task of creating and
updating *GBBS Pro* 2.2 software. Additional thanks to Ervin "Skip" Thompson, Gene Buckle,
Henry Pedro, Kevin M. Smallwood, Andrew Wells, and Steve Funk for their contributions.

The "Dragon Chatting With a User" art on the cover was originally created
by Todd Helmenstine and Dick Sloan, and colorized by Brian Wiser.

The Cover and Book were designed by Brian Wiser.

PRODUCTION

Brian Wiser → Design, Layout, Editing, Proofreading
Bill Martens → Editing, Proofreading, Project Lead

DISCLAIMER

About the Producers

Brian Wiser

Brian Wiser is a producer of books, films, games, and events, as well as a long-time consultant, enthusiast and historian of Apple, the Apple II and Macintosh. Steve Wozniak and Steve Jobs were early influences, as well as magazines like *A+, Creative Computing, InCider,* and *Nibble.*

Brian designed, edited, and co-produced over 50 retro computer books including: *Nibble Viewpoints: Business Insights From The Computing Revolution, Cyber Jack: The Adventures of Robert Clardy and Synergistic Software, Synergistic Software: The Early Games, The Apple's Apprentice, The Colossal Computer Cartoon Book: Enhanced Edition, Graphically Speaking: Enhanced Edition, What's Where in the Apple: Enhanced Edition,* and *The WOZPAK: Special Edition* – an important Apple II historical book with Steve Wozniak's restored original, technical handwritten notes. Brian is also the author of *The Etch-a-Sketch and Other Fun Programs.*

He passionately preserves and archives all facets of Apple's history, and noteworthy companies such as Beagle Bros and Applied Engineering, featured on AppleArchives.com. His writing, interviews and books are featured on the technology news site CallApple.org and in *Call-A.P.P.L.E.* magazine that he co-produces as an A.P.P.L.E. board member. Brian also co-produced the retro iOS game *Structris.*

In 2004, Brian was cast as an extra in Joss Whedon's movie *Serenity*, leading him to being a producer / director for the documentary film *Done The Impossible: The Fans' Tale of Firefly & Serenity,* interviewing fans and cast, as well as recruiting Adam Baldwin to host it and Jewel Staite to voice-over the special features. He brought Ron Glass and other *Firefly* cast aboard his Browncoat Cruise convention and recruited several of the *Firefly* cast to appear in a film for charity.

For 25 years, he helped the monks of the Holy Trinity Abbey with their computers and became close friends with them. Brian wrote about that journey of friendship and discovery in a new, nontraditional book.

Throughout these experiences, he also develops close personal relationships with many actors, authors, and computer industry luminaries. Brian speaks about his adventures to large audiences at conventions around the country.

Bill Martens

Bill Martens is a systems engineer specializing in office infrastructures and has been programming since 1976. The DEC PDP 11/40 with ASR-33 Teletypes and CRT's were his first computing platforms along with the Apple II computer.

Bill worked for Apple Pugetsound Program Library Exchange (A.P.P.L.E.) under Val Golding and Dick Hubert as a data manager and programmer in the 1980s, and is the current president of the A.P.P.L.E. user group established in 1978. He reorganized A.P.P.L.E. and restarted Call-A.P.P.L.E. magazine in 2002, and is the production editor for the A.P.P.L.E. website callapple.org. Influences in Bill's computing life came from *Byte, Creative Computing,* and *Call-A.P.P.L.E.* magazines as well as his mentors Samuel Perkins, Don Williams, Joff Morgan, and Mike Christensen.

Bill is a co-author of the *Email III* system along with Michael Sly, which in 1982 implemented the first known instance of Instant Messaging and Group Conferencing in a Bulletin Board System (BBS) at Brablec High School in Roseville, Michigan (presumably before other IM systems). He is a co-producer of several dozen retro computing books including *What's Where in the Apple: Enhanced Edition, The WOZPAK: Special Edition, Nibble Viewpoints: Business Insights From The Computing Revolution*, and co-programmer for the iOS retro game *Structris*. He also created the *ApPilot/W1* Pilot programming environment for the Apple II, TRS-80, TI99/4A, and IBM 360.

Bill has written many technical and commentary articles which have appeared in user group newsletters and magazines such as *Call-A.P.P.L.E.* In the 1990s, he created *The Library 2.0*, a self-generating website database system which was used in creating an early version of the A.P.P.L.E. website's software library sections. He also created the generator for producing his numerous game emulation websites such as virtualapple.org, virtualatari.org, and gamezyte.com. Bill is also the founder and co-creator of many other websites including mecc.co and applearchives.com. He likes writing science fiction novels in his spare time, and is a retired Japan X-League (X1) football player.

CONTENTS

1. Overview, Support, Features

2. Installation & Configuration

3. Running the System & Commands

4. Utility Program Reference

5. ACOS Reference

6. Modifying the System

7. Shell Listing

8. Appendices

Connected at 2400 baud!

Ctrl-S Stop/Start Spacebar to Exit

You spent a long day away from home...
Dreaming of worlds unseen...
And digital treasure...

Welcome! You have just connected to:

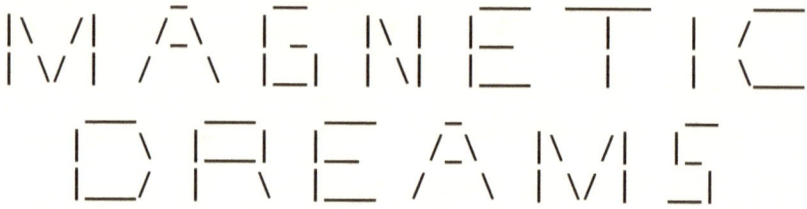

```
          >>>>>-- Magnetic Dreams BBS --<<<<<

   ******************************************
   *          Online Since 08/11/81         *
   *     Supporting: Apple II, IIGS, Amiga   *
   *      Message Bases, Online Games, Fun   *
   ******************************************

              1200/2400 Baud
          24 Hours a Day / 7 Days a Week
      Prometheus 2400  <>  Apple IIe  <>  10 Megabytes


      +-------------------------------------------+
      |         Call These Other Cool BBS's       |
      |                                           |
      |    <C><P><U>        Bitsko's Bar & Grill  |
      |    The Dock         Brimstone Manor       |
      |    S.O.B.           Lower Lights          |
      |    Twilight Zone    Motel West            |
      |    Woz Mania IIGS   Mystic Realms         |
      +---------/\------------------/\------------+
```

Enter your Account Number or "NEW" for New User:
-->

Introduction

by Brian Wiser

When I think of BBS's, one of the first things that comes to mind is the sound of my modem connecting to another computer and taking me to another world. And that's what they did – they took me and countless others to a world that the majority of people had no concept of in the 1980s. It allowed us to do such novel things as exchange electronic mail, share ideas by posting messages, learn about a variety of subjects, and play online games – long before the Internet was used by the public.

Using my Apple II computer, an external Prometheus ProModem 2400, and a program like *ASCII Express* or *ProTerm*, my computer could dial a phone number and connect to another computer running BBS (Bulletin Board System) software. After some modem screeching as the two computers were connecting, the magic began.

On the preceding page is a welcome screen for a BBS that I always wanted to create, but never did. Imagine the text slowly appearing word by word and line by line, on a monitor that was only capable of displaying green. After connecting, a BBS normally introduced its name and theme, supported computers and connection speeds, hours of operation, storage capacity, and other BBS's to call. Ultimately, the option was presented to login with an account or create a new one. Most people used a fun, weird or rebellious-sounding alias, rather than their real name. This was, after all, like the Wild West.

BBS's were usually run by hobbyists, both adults and kids – people like you and me. Sure, in the 1980s there were national commercial BBS's like CompuServe, Delphi, GEnie (General Electric), and Prodigy that were prohibitively expensive – charging as little as $6 per hour in the evenings to $30+ per hour during the day. Eventually, America Online (AOL) and eWorld (Apple) emerged too. The real fun was on home-grown BBS's! Hobbyists would buy software like *GBBS Pro* and turn their sometimes lonely computer into a public Bulletin Board System. They were purely text-based with no graphics or pictures to look at, apart from using text characters to create "ASCII art." Later in the 1980s, color text known as "ANSI art" became popular and many cult artists were born – spurring competitions and creating amazing BBS text art.

Finding BBS's to call with your modem wasn't the easiest thing at first. You'd get a BBS number from a friend and call to see what it was all about. Especially in the early days, there were no lists in magazines to refer to. Usually, each BBS had a list of other numbers to call. Upon connecting to a handful of Bulletin Board Systems, when I wasn't dodging busy signals preventing my entry, I learned of other BBS's whose numbers were posted. And thus, my exploration of the online world began – finding new friends and expanding my mind with the knowledge of what was *and* what could be.

In many ways, BBS's made me feel like I had opened a science fiction novel and found a secret key to a door that most people didn't know existed. And thinking of them today, my feelings haven't changed. I consider myself very lucky to have experienced BBS's in all their glory.

Dialing numbers and experiencing new BBS's for the first time was fun, random exploration. I'd normally call local BBS's, because calling out of state incurred incredibly expensive long-distance phone charges. It was something I did for a few hours every day, posting public messages, exchanging email, and playing text-based games like *Trade Wars* while tying up our phone line.

Occasionally, the sysop (system operator) who ran the BBS would break into chat while you were exploring their BBS – it was thrilling to be unexpectedly typing to another human in real-time. Outside of BBS's, there was no text chatting available and certainly nothing as novel as an instant message to a mobile phone – remember this was the early 1980s. Sysops were certainly god-like in their ability to grant access to "elite" areas, or smite people they didn't like by limiting access or deleting their account.

It's important to know that BBS's were typically "closed" systems – your account, email and public messages were only available to users of that particular BBS. BBS's were not usually networked together and typically could only have one user online at a time –

hence lots of busy signals for people trying to connect. As a result, users had a time limit of around 20 minutes per call before they were automatically disconnected. You had to prioritize – what were you going to do with your limited time? Anyone who was serious about running a BBS bought a dedicated phone line so it would be available 24 hours a day. Although, some were only available in the evening when parents wouldn't mind their only phone line being tied up by their kid's hobby, and the family computer being used exclusively for a BBS and nothing else.

And since BBS's were run by individuals, they were all a little different – both in the menu design and in the computers and subjects they catered to. BBS's were often aimed at fans of a specific computer brand (Apple, Atari, Commodore, IBM, Mac) who exchanged knowledge and software. They were *the* place to share computer tips, ideas, rumors of what new computers or programs were coming out, along with virtually any subject imaginable. And BBS's were a great place to make new friends, communicating through email and public messages. After all, we shared many interests in common! Hobbyists could choose different BBS software to use, and often customized the look and menu wording for more fun.

I miss the classic BBS days of the 1980s, but surprisingly they are still around! A few traditional dial-up BBS's are accessible via modems, and many more are on the Internet via Telnet and SSH protocols. Lists of BBS's can be found on websites like: https://www.telnetbbsguide.com.

In recent years, Bill Martens and I wanted *GBBS Pro* to be more accessible and legally available, so that BBS's could experience more of a resurgence. *GBBS Pro* is an Apple II program that's still used today by enthusiasts, despite being written in 1980.

So, we spoke with the software copyright holder Kevin M. Smallwood and learned that he felt exactly the same way. Kevin subsequently made *GBBS Pro* available through the GPL 3.0 License, and approved our site as the official place to download software and other resources: https://gbbs.applearchives.com.

We worked with programmer Lane Roathe who reconstructed the source code. Lane and Paul H. Lee spent significant time fixing many outstanding issues with the software, resulting in the new 2.2 version. Steve Funk recovered SuperTAC, ExFer, and other extensions.

Starting with a scan of the original *GBBS Pro* 2.1 manual from 1990, courtesy of Henry Pedro, Bill Martens and I corrected mistakes in the original documents. All documents were edited for grammar, formatting, and clarity. I also designed the new cover and the book.

Deleted content has been restored such as configurations, the glossary, and contribution credits that were only found in older manual versions. Fun cartoon art from Todd Helmenstine and Dick Sloan, that was only part of the *GBBS Pro* 1.0 manual, is included and also featured on the cover with newly-added color. The result is a new resource that is clearer, more complete, and easier to use.

We have a foreword from Kevin M. Smallwood, who has been very supportive of this book and our shared goal of reinvigorating people to embrace and connect with BBS's again with updated *GBBS Pro* software. Additional forewords from Andrew Wells, Gene Buckle, Ervin "Skip" Thompson, and Bill Martens give perspective on running BBS's. There is a new "Internet Setup Guide" by Gene Buckles, and Henry Pedro provided installation details that I merged with the existing "Initial System Configuration" chapter.

Beyond this new book and new software, *GBBS* has a long history that should not be forgotten. *GBBS* is the creation of Greg Schaefer, first released in 1980 as the *GBBS II Bulletin Board System*. We thank Greg for starting this journey. Thanks also go to Lance Taylor-Warren and Andrew Wells for their significant expansion of *GBBS Pro* up to 1993. In our new "GBBS History" section, you can read more about the history and see who has contributed to *GBBS* over the years.

It is our hope that this new *GBBS Pro* book will give readers a bit of nostalgia, and serve as inspiration and a tool to resurrect old BBS's and make new systems available. We hope to see all of you online!

Brian Wiser
January 2023

Kevin M. Smallwood

There and Back Again

I was an ambitious teenager who was always looking for a challenge. School was difficult for me because I didn't need six weeks to master a subject. Teachers grew impatient with me and my parents were understandably frustrated.

In 1980, several life-changing events began to unfold. The Commodore VIC-20 was released. The next year, *Donkey Kong* swept the nation. I was in awe of the technology. I would bug my dad to the point of exasperation for quarters so I could ride my bike to 7-11 and play. Understandably, he grew tired of this. A friend of mine had a VIC-20, so I rode my bike to his house after school and we would write our own games. Our first venture was called *Catacombs*. It was a text-based RPG with random hit points per opponent. We also recreated the 1979 classic *Lunar Lander*.

I showed this to my father who was impressed. He went to the local Apple store and bought a fully loaded Apple IIe with an 80-column card, memory expansion and two 5.25" drives. We didn't know why we would need it, but my dad and I subsequently purchased a Hayes Micromodem.

It was at this time when I discovered *Net-Works II* by Nick Naimo. Shortly thereafter, I came across *AE Pro* by United Software Artists. I knew this was something I had to be involved in. I ran a *Net-Works II* BBS but I had to hide it. My dad had told me he didn't want the phone ringing day and night. I disconnected the phone and ran the line to the modem. Problem solved! Dad eventually discovered that he wasn't receiving calls, but by this point he also saw the work I'd put into rewriting my BBS.

He bought me an Apple IIGS with a Mockingboard, TransWarp GS, and a Sider hard drive. This is when I discovered *GBBS*. It was the clear successor to *Net-Works II*. I wiped my hard drive and dedicated it to *GBBS*. ACOS was amazing. I was self-taught when it came to coding. ACOS made sense to me and I loved it. After a lot of coaxing, I convinced Lance P. Taylor-Warren (of L&L Productions) to allow me to invest in the company and run a sister site. I subsequently purchased *ExFer* and released updates on a regular basis. The amazing Andy Nicholas wrote *SuperTAC* to give *GBBS* an "*AE Pro*" look and feel.

We were kids. We didn't know what we could or could not do, but we loved every minute of it. Eventually, technology passed us by and our lives as young adults brought new demands. *GBBS* went into maintenance mode and passed through a few hands.

In 2006, I purchased the rights to *GBBS* outright. I already owned *ExFer* from an acquisition in the 1990s, and I also acquired the rights to *Net-Works II* from Mr. Naimo. I didn't buy them for monetary purposes – I bought them because they were the bedrock of my career in technology. Bulletin Boards had messaging, forums, databases, file systems, code and more. Every one of these technologies are a part of my daily life. I still write code (PowerShell resembles ACOS if you ask me), and I deploy and manage databases and messaging solutions. Bulletin Boards gave me the educational foundation that school never could.

This brings us to the present day. *GBBS*, *ExFer*, *SuperTAC* and *Net-Works II* need to be available to everyone. It's my hope that they can teach people the amazing lessons that they taught me. I'll say to my peers that "I get it." These systems are engrained in our childhood. We grew up with them and are proud of our contributions. Every BBS was different. Some were terrible, but they were "ours" and we were proud to have people call in. They were micro-social networks.

Please enjoy using these applications. I hope they bring you as much joy as they've brought me.

Kevin M. Smallwood
February 2017

Andrew Wells

Back in the late 1970s is when I found computers – more specifically, the Apple II. I'd heard of a new computer store and stopped by to visit, and became pretty much a fixture there. I did some tech work for them, including building some S-100 bus cards for IMSAI. I saw a few other computers too, but none really kept my attention like the Apple did.

While there, the store owners decided they wanted a BBS. I don't remember which one they settled on, but I pretty much kept it going as acting sysop. I met AJ Cohen, a member of the Apple II Enthusiasts group on Facebook, there as well. It's funny how small the world is, and that more than 30 years later we ran across each other on Facebook. The owners later closed the store as they planned to open another one that wasn't a franchised store.

I started calling some of the BBSs around town during that time, and continued doing so afterward. A Dial-Your-Match (DYM) sysop and I became friends, and when the Apple Cat II 212 board came out, I wrote the 1200 baud driver for his system.

Then I decided to run my own system, The Connection, that I started with Applesoft with a few routines in machine language. The first version went online in July of 1984. The Connection was run on an Enhanced IIe, Apple HD20SC, 3.5" and 5.25" drives, 1MB Slinky memory card, ThunderClock Plus, and a Hayes Smartmodem 2400 connected to an Apple Super Serial Card.

The original version was pretty simple. It didn't have the capabilities I wanted, so I kept adding to it. Some of the functions required more capabilities than Applesoft had, so I kept adding to the machine language. Added to the modem control routines were string handling commands that were available in other languages and other BASIC languages. File handling was also done through machine language as it was much faster. The Connection was inclusive – gender, lifestyle, sexual orientation or identity were accepted by anyone using the system. Any indication of bias, and those people

were ejected. Luckily most BBS users at the time were open-minded.
I met my ex-wife through The Connection as well.

In the meantime, I started hearing about *GBBS Pro*. In looking
at it, I saw that it had most of what I could want in a BBS program.
Along with the easily-modified segments, it was also easy to write
new segments. The Connection went live using *GBBS Pro 1.2* around
October of 1987. Included on the system were the usual things that are
part of the base *GBBS Pro* system. Additionally, there was a matching
system similar to DYM.

After running it awhile, I started seeing people reporting bugs.
I checked them out myself and confirmed most of them. However,
by this time the original author had pretty much quit supporting it.
Because of this, and the desire to fix the problems, I disassembled the
ACOS kernel. While others had patches out to fix some of the bugs,
others were more complicated and required re-assembling the code,
hence the disassembly.

Sometime within the next year, L&L Productions purchased
GBBS Pro. However, they didn't have the most recent build of the
code. I was contacted by them regarding the code and support for
ACOS/*GBBS Pro*. The first official release with L&L was 1.3j. After
some updates and further fixes, 2.0 was released, then 2.11, and 2.14.
Also during this time, the next generation was being written – initially
called *LLUCE*. That one was my pet, and it was getting to be pretty
solid by 1993. However, L&L seemed to have lost interest. Not too
surprising since Apple wasn't really supporting the II series by then.

During the maintenance and updating of ACOS and the
development of *LLUCE*, we had several beta testers and a few who
wrote code. Andy Nicholas wrote most of the modem drivers, all of
which were converted for *LLUCE*, some of which I had to alter for
interrupt handling.

Kevin Smallwood also was a part of all this as well. I was not
surprised to hear he had purchased the rights to both *GBBS* and
LLUCE. After acquisition, it appeared that the disks with the software
on them, especially the source code, were damaged. I never saw them,
so don't know if they were beyond recovery or not.

After acquiring some hardware, including an Apple IIGS ROM 3, and making sure I had reliable power supplies and 3.5" drives, I started going through my disks. I found multiple copies of ACOS 2.11 and 2.14 and *LLUCE*. All the disks needed were still there and were good, except one disk had one bad block, but that one was a backup, so all was good.

Andrew Wells
July 2017

Gene Buckle

I don't recall where I heard about BBS's initially, but it was some time in 1983 – shortly after getting a VIC-20 as payment for writing a (really bad) game for *Commander Magazine*. After much begging, pleading, and cajoling, my mother finally bought me my first modem – a VIC-1600. The VIC-1600 was a 300 baud modem that had no direct connection to the phone line. When you wanted to dial out, you manually dialed your phone and when the other side answered and gave a carrier tone, you'd quickly unplug the tiny RJ-22 connector from your handset and jam it into the socket on the VIC-1600. Suffice to say that it wasn't long before the little latching tab on that end of the cord broke, much to my mother's displeasure.

The first BBS I called was an Apple II BBS called Dair Lair in Puyallup, WA, run by a guy named Dasturdly Gonzueala. I was user #149 on that system and I was hooked from the first menu prompt. That system led me to more systems and those led me to even more. By the time 1986 rolled around, I was cooking along at 1200 baud (auto-dial!) and called over 100 different systems a week. The Pacific Northwest was an amazing place to be if you were a BBS addict – there were easily 200 systems within the local calling distance I had.

I wasn't much into games, but no BBS program or utility download was safe from my virtual fingers. I didn't have the wherewithal to run a BBS myself yet, but by god I was going to know *everything* there was about BBSes and how they worked – often times to the derision of my peers and the annoyance of more than one sysop.

I had it in my head that I wanted to be a programmer as a career, and BBSes were a neat collection of the building blocks required for just about any kind of application you'd care to create. You had to learn about database design, user interface design, networking (eventually), and serial communication and protocols. I probably built hundreds of frameworks that helped me master each one of those disciplines, but for whatever reason, never released a full BBS program of my own. The things I learned have proven invaluable though – 2017 marks my 31st anniversary as a professional programmer.

The heyday of the Bulletin Board System is long gone, but it has become a small and vibrant community of enthusiasts who enjoy doing things "old school" – not because it's any better than what we've got now, it's just different enough to be enjoyable.

I can't recall which I got first – *GBBS Pro* or an Apple IIe – this was back in the summer or fall of 2008. I know that I'd decided that I wanted to put another board up on vintage hardware. Previously I had a Heathkit H-89 running *Citadel* that was on a phone line as opposed to being on the Internet. The lack of callers couldn't justify the wear and tear on the machine, so I took it down after a few months.

The Apple IIe was one that had been upgraded to the Enhanced model. I added a No Slot Clock, a Super Serial Card, and a Focus IDE controller to the system in order to make it usable as a BBS host.

The Internet interface consisted of a modem "emulator" called *tcpser* that was written by Jim Brain. The basic idea with *tcpser* is that you run it on either a Windows or Linux host and connect your vintage machine to the host computer via a null modem cable. As far as the computer on the other end was concerned, it was talking to a standard Hayes compatible modem.

It turned out that *tcpser* had an issue with setup – if you used a *nix telnet client when "calling," the system would double-echo everything you typed. This happened because the telnet client didn't get a special control sequence from the host that basically said, "I'll echo input so you don't do that." Consequently, everything you typed ccaaammmee oouutt lliikkee tthhiiss. I updated *tcpser* so that upon connecting it would send out the "I'll echo!" sequence.

The copy of *GBBS Pro* I had included (somehow, I don't recall the details) a snapshot of a game called *Land of Spur* that had been used by a local Tacoma, Washington BBS called Dura-Europos. I did some small additional configuration to the system and put it online as Age of Reason in 2008. It caused quite a stir at the time as it was the only, and possibly first, Apple IIe BBS ever put up on the Internet using real hardware.

I soon discovered that v1.3j of *GBBS Pro* wasn't so keen on understanding dates past the turn of the century – the Y2K problem. I found that if I set the date to 1987, it would match the current year the BBS was running at – 2009 at this point. It went very well with the age of the hardware if nothing else. :)

The BBS had a few calls a month for its entire time online, which all things considered, wasn't that bad. A bad storm killed the original machine's power supply, but that was fairly quickly rectified.

Unfortunately in the fall of 2011, I was diagnosed with Stage 3 lung cancer and by 2012, didn't have the energy to spend on the board any longer. Since my chances of survival at that point were unknown, I handed the hardware over to a friend for him to enjoy – he really loved the *Land of Spur* game and was doing research into porting it to other vintage platforms.

I've since survived my cancer and recently got the IIe back that my BBS ran on. Age of Reason is currently back online and accepting new users, so who knows what the future brings? :)

Gene Buckle
February 2017

telnet://aor.retroarchive.org:2300

```
The Age of Reason BBS
Running GBBS Pro v1.3
2400 Baud, 8 Bits, 1 Stop
Proudly run by geneb
```

Ervin "Skip" Thompson

I first started my BBS in October 1986. Those were the days when normal folks looked at you funny if you mentioned you had a computer. The local BBS scene was dominated by *C-Net* running at 300 baud on Commodore 64 computers, and inhabited by colorful characters going by handles such as Killer-Bunny, Xevious, and Athena Bright Eyes. We met for Pizza Bashes at local pizza restaurants, and occasionally at a sysop's house for a party.

I had an Apple IIe computer and wanted to be one of these mystical sysops, and I discovered a BBS program for the Apple IIe called *GBBS Pro*. It had a peculiar application language that appeared similar to BASIC that allowed me to program the board to my heart's content. As I was between wives at the time, and really enjoyed programming, this provided an attractive alternative to spending evenings in a bar. I spent many happy hours developing code for the board. Installing a RAM drive let me keep programming and have the board back online by the second or third ring when someone called.

Being something of a Roman history buff, I decided to name my board Dura-Europos after an ancient city that suffered a tragic fate at the hands of those "dastardly Persians." My original board was setup as a story board, where users took on various personas, "walked" around to different locations (message boards), and participated in role-playing stories. The theme of the board was an ancient Roman city with lots of fantasy mixed in. The Persians made a convenient villain.

The story format was quite successful for a period, often logging over 50 messages a day – but alas, nothing is forever. The story board fell into decline after a while as users lost interest. In an effort to keep the board viable, I modernized it, creating "New Dura" while retaining the original board as "Old Dura." Users could use the version they preferred, and most new users preferred the new version. This revitalized the board for a while, but soon the Internet raised its ugly head (cue scary music). I took the board down on or after April 1993 after making a complete backup.

Then in early 2016, I stumbled on the YouTube video "Running a Telnet BBS on an Apple IIe Using a Raspberry Pi" recorded by Lon.TV and was fascinated. This guy was describing running an Apple IIe BBS via Telnet. Gadzooks! I watched the video over and over, taking screenshots of his Super Serial Card's DIP switches, etc. The result of was that I relaunched Dura-Europos in February of 2016, and have been relearning the charming programming language used by *GBBS Pro v1.2.*

The current incarnation of the BBS is running on a vintage Platinum Apple IIe. The components were rescued from eBay and also include an Applied Engineering TimeMaster Clock card, Applied Engineering Transwarp accelerator, two Super Serial cards, and a Kensington System Saver. Modern components are the CFFA 3000 compact flash card, a Raspberry Pi running *tcpser* modem simulator and a flat screen monitor. I currently do development in Windows using *AppleWin*, then transfer it to the Apple using *ADTPro* via one of the Super Serial cards.

Ervin "Skip" Thompson
February 2017

telnet://dura-bbs.net:6359

Welcome to

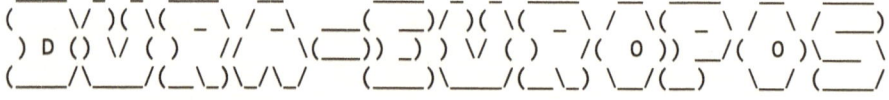

```
 ___ __  _ __  _  ___         ___  ___  _  ___  _  ___ __  _ _  ___
(   \/ )( \(  _ \ / _\  __(  _)/ )( \(  _ \ / \( _ \ / \ /  _)
 ) D () \/ ()   //   \(__)) _) ) \/ ()  /( 0 )) _/( 0 )\__ \
(___/\___/(_\_)\_/\_/    (___)\___/(_\_) \_/(_)  \_/ (___/
```

Built with GBBS Pro BBS software.
Originally on-line from 1986-1993.
Resurrected from backup disks and placed on the internet in 2016.

Bill Martens

The Real World

I began programming in 1976 on a DEC PDP 11/4 system in Nuremberg, Germany. Having been the product of a military family, I was given the choice of either taking computer classes or taking algebra. The algebra teacher was not one of my favorite teachers, thus I choose computer classes even though I really didn't have an affinity for computers.

Funny enough, I was one of those people who believed that computers took too much time from living, and that point rings ever more true today. We have reached the point where we can't seem to live without our computers and devices, and we sure can't survive without them in the real business world.

It was with this frame of mind that I set out programming. My first contact with an Apple computer came in the form of ads for the Apple-1 computer in *Creative Computing* magazine's October 1976 issue. While I was never aware that this was the future, as soon as I settled on the Apple-1 as my go to machine, the Apple II came out with ads in almost every major computer magazine at the time. There were only three – *Dr. Dobbs Journal*, *Creative Computing*, and *Byte*.

This computer would change the world and my life. In fact, it would dominate my life for the next 14 years with the first break from it coming finally in 1990. It was that year that I moved to Japan and basically gave up everything Apple II and BBS related. But I am getting ahead of myself here by a long shot.

In 1977, network communications were limited to those who were connected to Usenet via an educational institution's mainframe or one of the military computers. Where I was, the only communication we did was via a teletype terminal on a hard-cabled network of machines.

When the Apple II computer came out, it really wasn't much of a communications machine, and it really wasn't until 300 baud modems came out that the realm of possibilities began to open up. When I went to A.P.P.L.E. in 1980, they were just getting started with their BBS and Val Golding was pushing people involved in the setup to get it up and running. Don Williams, Darrell and Ron Aldrich, Bob Clardy and others there at A.P.P.L.E. were working with an in-house modem box developed by the Aldrich brothers and were ahead of the curve when it came to modems. Sales of the box also allowed group members to connect and communicate with the BBS via their Apple II's.

While it was nice to finally be able to communicate with others via the computer, it was still extremely rudimentary with communications limited to what the system could handle with the homebrew modem box and an Apple II computer with two floppies.

However, this was still pretty much the state of my own system when I started The Hack Shack BBS in Seattle in 1984. I owned a 300 baud Micromodem and ran the BBS on an Apple II Plus. Occasionally, I hooked up a Hayes 1200 baud modem which I borrowed from a friend for a spell until I purchased my own.

The software I ran was a highly-modified version of *Apple-Net* BBS with many new functions and several fixes applied. By the time I completed my BBS, it almost resembled a completely different system and was actually a lot safer because I had closed several of the security holes which existed in the original system.

One such security hole was pressing Ctrl-D during a text input session, which allowed users to break out of the BBS software remotely and then drop them to the Applesoft BASIC prompt. They could then type INIT HELLO and wipe out your BBS in a matter of minutes. Although *Apple-Net* was not the only BBS software with this problem, it was one of the most well-known ones.

I continued to modify the software, upgrade the system and began adding floppy drives in order to allow for more users on the system and more messages. I added Drives 3 and 4 which gave me an additional 280K of disk space. The next thing I knew, the BBS had grown to 150 users.

The one thing that seemed to take more time than making modifications to the system, was that it was limited to one user at a time. That meant that if the line was busy when you tried to call the local BBS, you had to try again later just like a normal phone call. The difference was that once you got connected, you could send mail to any of the users on the system and post messages to the public bulletin area.

This openness is what really created the Internet as we know it today. It was the desire for more openness as well as the desire to put more information online for the users to view which meant that every advance during the BBS age seemed to head more and more towards the ultimate network.

Around 1984, many BBS sysops began to develop systems that could exchange message bases and soon the world began to get closer and closer. These interconnecting systems were mostly developed by the local area BBS operators. It was a concerted effort in many cases with sysops getting together and deciding the required items for each system and the coordinated dialup and update time which would be used to exchange the messages. This led to much of the UUCP style systems which existed by 1986.

By the time I moved to Auburn, Washington in 1985, The Hack Shack BBS had grown to over 300 users and was still on a four drive system. This would change very drastically after I moved, as Video Technology Corporation of Hong Kong produced the Laser 128EX in 1987, which was a 3.4MHz clone of the new Apple IIc computer. This machine was a definite game changer for my little BBS.

With this faster, cheaper computer, I put my entire system on a single floppy disk. With 800K on the floppy and another 1 megabyte on the RAM card, I suddenly had a system which rivaled the speed of those who had hard drives – at half the cost.

Although I did not have many of the resources on my BBS found on many other sites of the time, my system did have one of the very first sources of information in the United States for ski resorts, road conditions, and weather, as well as many technical and programming documents for the Apple II.

One advance which allowed for many changes in the BBS was the introduction of *GBBS Pro 1.2* by Greg Schaeffer. This easily-changed system was programmed via the ACOS language and resembled BASIC in many respects. After looking at systems like *ProTree BBS*, *ModemWorks BBS*, and several others, it seemed that none of the BBS's could match the flexibility of the ACOS language. So I switched and instantly began to alter my system with mods from other boards and some I developed myself.

What I was left with was a system that took only about 200K and would leave almost 1600K for uploads and downloads. It seemed that no matter what I added, nothing would make it take more space. My BBS was the ultimate containing modifications such as *Macos*, *SuperTac AE*, and other major mods – the power and scope of the system would rival any Web site created today.

The Hack Shack BBS became the Information Station BBS in 1987 as the times changed from the Apple II computer being just a hobby and hacking machine to being a professionally-used computer in places of business. The information perspective had become king with stock trading systems and how-to guides being more relevant to the computer using public. While the software trading BBS's still existed, they were slowing losing out to BBS's which had more online games and information.

The wonderful thing about *GBBS Pro* was that components of the system, or segments, were available to all system operators at the time through every *GBBS* system around. Without this trading of segments, ACOS would have been just another language in the more than 2,300 programming languages around the world. The availability of segments, both free and paid, led to very complex *GBBS Pro* systems and eventually to those with graphical menus and welcome splash screens.

I ran my BBS's until I moved in 1989. I can still remember the day that I began moving, and had to shut down my BBS. This was indeed a sad day as it meant the end of an era in my life. Having over 500 users by this time, I considered the Apple II computer and the BBS had its heyday, and that my family responsibilities dictated that I should get on with life. It was only after I moved to Japan and started to re-connect with the global community, that I recognized that many people tried to keep the BBS community alive on Apple IIGS systems until about 1995.

There is one interesting common theme that came out of the different groups of people in the BBS world. Many of them went on to the Internet with early adoption and even eagerness to expand into that realm. While this is not necessarily a classification of people, it is interesting to look back at these groups and see who they were before they became the Internet personalities that they are today.

The first group was the younger kids. They were the ones who knew all the tricks to shut down the systems, and went out of their way to irritate every person on the BBS – leading the sysop to shut them out of the system.

The second group was the high school and college kids. They were the most aggressive with their ideas and the things that they did. Many of the hacking boards were run by this age group, in spite of the fact that many of them could have gone to jail if it occurred today.

The next group was the computer gurus. This group encapsulated those who had seen it all – the system operators themselves, software developers, or other computer industry-related people. They were the ones who knew how to fix the problems, had the technical specifications of almost any item known, and were more than forthcoming in giving the information to anyone who wanted it.

The final group was the newbies. This group seemed to be lost in a cloud. No matter how many times you would tell them how to do something, they didn't seem to be able to figure out how to perform the same task a second time without bugging the system operator for more help.

While all of these groups had their own merits and social demerits, people often overlooked the basic idea of the BBS – to bring people from all walks of life together and to facilitate communication between people.

In retrospect, the 1980s were definitely the time when the world began to get closer together and talk with each other. BBS's were the first step of the real gathering of the peoples of the world that we see today with the Internet and social networking.

Today, the spirit of the BBS world of the 1980s has all but been forgotten in the wild Internet climate. It is our hope that this book will allow those in the community old enough to remember those days to reminisce a bit, while giving the younger generation a taste of what we went through to communicate back then.

Bill Martens
March 2017


```
:::::::::::::::::::::::::::::::::::::
:              GBBS Pro V2.2              :
:::::::::::::::::::::::::::::::::::::

        The A.P.P.L.E. Crate BBS

        Awaiting call 1 on 04/01/76
        This will be call 1 today
```

CHAPTER 1

Overview, Support, Features

A Little About GBBS Pro

GBBS Pro is a complete Bulletin Board System (BBS), which uses a totally new concept in the area of communications. It offers the most diverse and advanced features of any communications system on the market. *GBBS Pro* is so advanced that it comes as a complete system that can be configured and run by a novice, yet can challenge the most advanced programmer.

It uses an "All Purpose Communication Operating System" (ACOS) which is a self-contained language with its own proprietary compiler. *GBBS Pro* can be custom-tailored to your specifications and easily modified through the ACOS language. The ACOS language may also be used to support other communication based applications you may wish to program, and yet is very powerful by itself.

Dear GBBS Pro User

Thank you for downloading *GBBS Pro* from the official Web site: https://gbbs.applearchives.com. With the *GBBS Pro* diskette images, you have received the state-of-the-art in bulletin board communication systems. *GBBS Pro* is a user-friendly and highly-modifiable system. You can easily alter it to satisfy your individual BBS needs. It is my sincere hope that *GBBS Pro* meets your high standards for software excellence.

Sincerely,

Kevin M. Smallwood
Owner of *GBBS Pro* Copyrights
February 2017

Terms of Usage / Disclaimer

GBBS Pro is intended for use on as many computer systems as you wish. While the original program was intended for one copy per computer, this software is now under GPL 3.0 licensing. *GBBS Pro* is copyrighted, distributable to all, and free for use by everyone. *GBBS Pro* is not public domain. Using one copy on more than one computer is allowed and encouraged.

Kevin M. Smallwood and Apple Pugetsound Program Library Exchange (A.P.P.L.E.) make no warranties, either expressed or implied, toward the *GBBS Pro* software package, this book, quality, performance or usefulness towards an application. All items are provided "as-is." While all possible steps have been taken to ensure that the information included within is accurate, the publisher, authors, and Kevin M. Smallwood assume no responsibility for any errors or omissions, or for damages resulting from the use of the information contained herein.

GBBS Website: Software Updates, Mailing List

The Official *GBBS Pro* Web site https://gbbs.applearchives.com features software enhancements and fixes for any bugs that might be found, as well as additional resources. Sign up for the GBBS Mailing List to receive upgrade notices.

You may leave questions in the Q&A section. Someone will attempt to answer questions relevant to the software as soon as possible. Please save this route as a last resort.

Technical Support

The "GBBS Support & Sysops Exchange" was a special bulletin board run by previous owners for sysops to call, ask questions, and exchange ideas, modifications, and information. This support system from 1990 is no longer available. Technical support is only provided by the Apple II community at large.

Modifications to GBBS

Modifications made to *GBBS Pro* software that are posted publicly make up one of the greatest assets of the system. You may share any modification that you have made to your system, but doing so puts the modification in the public domain. Anyone who has access to the modification can and may freely use the modification.

If you do not want your modifications used by others, then please do not post them. Ideas and concepts, such as using word wrap in email, can also be copied by other sysops. Sysops can use the same ideas to write their own code to get the same results. Sharing is encouraged, as ideas improve when people share them and make them even better!

System Requirements

Computer – Any Apple II series computer with at least 64K of memory and two floppy drives. It supports both upper and lowercase, and most 80-column cards.

Storage – most storage types are supported, including 5.25" floppy disk drives, the Apple 3.5" drive, most fixed and removable hard drives, and solid state media. At least one Mass Storage device is recommended. A 3.5" 800K floppy disk is considered mass storage for the purposes of this installation.

Modem – 300 to 38400 baud modems are supported. Internal modem card support includes the Hayes MicroModem, Zoom Modem IIe, and Apple CAT 103 or 212. External modems are supported with a Super Serial Card or IIc/IIGS serial port.

Clock – If a clock is not used, the system will estimate the time for you. Clock add-ons are supported like the Applied Engineering Timemaster II H.O., Thunderclock (and compatibles), and SMT's popular "No Slot Clock."

Printer – A printer is not required, but most printers are supported, including popular serial and parallel port cards.

GBBS History

GBBS II was created in 1980 by Greg Schaefer. *GBBS Pro* and the ACOS language were originally developed and released by Greg Schaefer in 1985. The software was sold to L&L Productions in 1986 with further development performed by Lance Taylor-Warren and Andrew Wells from 1986 to 1993.

Kevin M. Smallwood purchased the rights in 2006, and in 2013 announced that *GBBS Pro* would be placed under GPL 3.0 licensing. In 2017, spearheaded by Brian Wiser and Bill Martens of Call-A.P.P.L.E., Kevin approved the official *GBBS* Web site https://gbbs.applearchives.com to distribute *GBBS Pro* and related resources. This expanded and redesigned book was created. In 2019, a newly-compiled and updated 2.2 version was released.

GBBS Software Major Releases

II	1980	GS Software	Greg Schaefer
II 1.7	1983	GS Software	Greg Schaefer
Pro 1.0	1985	GS Software	Greg Schaefer
Pro 1.3	1986	GS Software	Greg Schaefer
Pro 1.3j	1987	L&L Productions	Lance Taylor-Warren
Pro 2.0	1990	L&L Productions	Lance Taylor-Warren
Pro 2.14	1993	L&L Productions	Lance Taylor-Warren
Pro 2.2	2018	A.P.P.L.E.	Kevin M. Smallwood

Program Development

II	Greg Schaefer
II 1.7	Greg Schaefer
Pro 1.0	Greg Schaefer

Pro 1.3   Greg Schaefer

Pro 1.3j   Greg Schaefer, Lance Taylor-Warren

Pro 2.0   Andrew Wells, Lance Taylor-Warren

Pro 2.2   Lane Roathe, Paul H. Lee

Additional Programming

Pro 1.3j   Scott Galbrath (external files), Gary Edwards

Pro 2.0   Andrew Wells (ACOS Kernel), Gary Edwards
             Andrew Nicholas (Protocol Driver files)

Pro 2.2   Henry Pedro, Bill Martens

Beta Testing

II 1.7   Ken Scrogan, Glenn Heyhurst

Pro 1.3j   Dave Hart, Keith Christian, Ron Gabbert, Mike Gola.

Pro 2.0   Steve Schnieder, Larry Hawkins, Kevin M. Smallwood,
             Adam Brown, Gary Edwards

Pro 2.2   Henry Pedro, Bill Martens, Antoine Vignau, Gene Buckle,
             Ervin "Skip" Thompson

Documentation

II 1.7   Bob Gaiser, Karen Schaefer

Pro 1.0   Bob Gaiser, Mike Gola, Greg Schaefer
             Illustrations – Todd Helmenstine, Dick Sloan

Pro 1.3   Greg Schacfer

Pro 1.3j   Lance Taylor-Warren, Lori Errico

Pro 2.0   Lance Taylor-Warren, Andrew Wells

Pro 2.2   Brian Wiser, Bill Martens, Gene Buckle, Henry Pedro

What's New in Version 2.2

As this software was originally written and updated in the 1980s and 1990s, we cannot guarantee that the system will function properly on modern computers. We encourage users to report any bugs discovered. General changes since version 2.14, released in 1993, are:

- Copyright update for Kevin M. Smallwood's GPL 3.0 Release.

- This new and expanded book.

- *GBBS* system segments updated.

- Source Code updated to simplify future updates.

- Various bug fixes for improved reliability:
  a. SSC driver
  b. Modem driver

Getting Started

CHAPTER 2

Installation & Configuration

Configuring the System

Getting your system up and running is a matter of three simple steps. If you follow these instructions, your board should be up and running in half an hour or less!

1. Make a backup of your *GBBS Pro* master disks or your downloaded disk images, found at: https://gbbs.applearchives.com

   Disk 1 – GBBS.CONFIG
   Disk 2 – GBBS.SYSTEM

2. Configure *GBBS Pro* to your hardware setup.

3. Insert the appropriate data for your BBS system and name your BBS.

4. Start running your BBS.

* IMPORTANT *

Before going any further, please complete step one by making a backup of both sides of the *GBBS Pro* master diskette, or disk images. Use any ProDOS-based copier (e.g. *ProDOS FILER*, *ProSel Volume Copy*, *Copy II Plus*) to copy the program disks. When you are finished, store the originals in a safe place, and only work with the duplicates.

Initial System Configuration

You will need a formatted ProDOS volume of at least 800K to successfully install *GBBS Pro*. Enter all the information as accurately as possible. If you modify your hardware configuration later, you can change the corresponding software configuration.

The first step in getting your bulletin board up and running is to tell *GBBS Pro* about your hardware setup. To do this, simply boot the GBBS.CONFIG disk. If you have a second 5.25" drive, insert the GBBS.SYSTEM disk. The disk will spin and you will then be asked if you wish to proceed with the configuration:

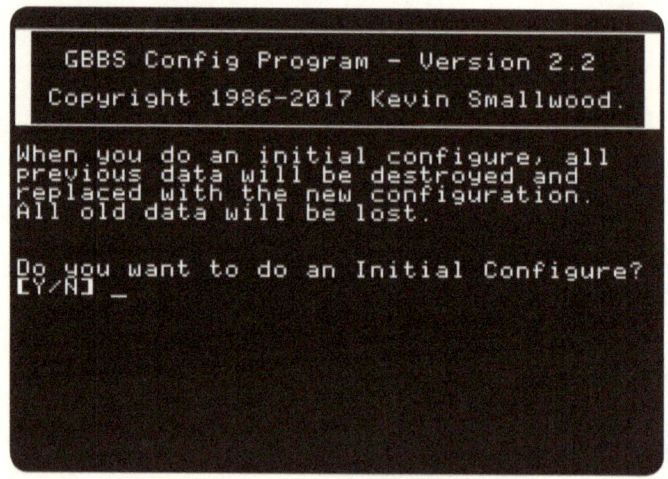

Answer "Y" to start a new installation and you will be prompted to answer several questions about your system.

Basic Questions

First, you will be asked to enter a name for your BBS system. Please note that commas or colons cannot be part of the name. Also, since the name is used in context such as "Welcome to", the first word of your name should be "The". For example, if the name of your system is National BBS, you should enter "The National BBS" as your system name. This way when a user logs on, they will be greeted with "Welcome to The National BBS" instead of "Welcome to National BBS".

Next, you will be asked to enter some information about yourself. First, you must enter your name. Next, you will be prompted to enter your phone number. Since this number may be made public to users, you may wish to type in your voice phone number so they may contact you to report any problems. If you do not want to use your voice phone number, type in the phone number of your system. Finally, you will be asked to enter your location, in the form of city and state.

You will then be prompted to enter a 4 to 8 character password that you will use to log on your system. This password can be whatever you choose, and can be composed of any characters. Take care, however, when making passwords. Be sure that the password isn't too easy to guess to avoid illegal entry by other users. After entering this password, you will be asked to enter a 1 to 20 character password that serves as a backup security system. When you call your system remotely from another computer you will be asked for this password to ensure that only you are allowed on your system as Sysop.

```
       GBBS Config Program - Version 2.2
       Copyright 1986-2017 Kevin Smallwood.

           - System Information -
    System Name: The A.P.P.L.E. Crate
    Sysop Name: Steve Wozniak
    Sysop Phone Number: 206-555-0000
    Sysop is From: SEATTLE,WA
    Logon Password:   TEST
    Remote Password: TEST01
    Is this information correct? [Y/N] _
```

Once you finish entering this data, the screen will clear, display what you entered, and ask you if the data is correct. If what you entered is correct, press "Y". If not, press "N" to begin again.

Video and Modem

The next screen allows you to enter your Video Driver for your Apple II model. Select the appropriate choice and press RETURN. Your 80 column card must be located in Slot 3, as this is the slot where *GBBS Pro* will always default.

```
            - Configure Video Driver -

     1 - Apple ][+ w/o lower case
     2 - Apple ][+ w/ lower case
     3 - Apple ][+ w/ Videx 80 col
     4 - Apple //e in 40 col mode
     5 - Apple //e in 80 col mode
     6 - Apple //c in 40 col mode
     7 - Apple //c in 80 col mode
     8 - Apple IIgs in 40 col mode
     9 - Apple IIgs in 80 col mode
   Which? [1-9] _
```

Next you are asked to select the type of Modem Driver or Serial Card interface you are using. Choosing "No Modem/Local Mode" will take you to the printer configuration screen.

```
           - Reconfigure Modem Driver -

     1 - No Modem/Local mode

     2 - Apple-Cat 103 - 300 baud
     3 - Apple-Cat 212 - 300/1200 baud
     4 - DC Hayes Micromodem II
     5 - Zoom Modem IIe

     6 - Epic 2400 Classic II
     7 - Applied Engineering DataLink 2400

     8 - Super Serial Card driver
     9 - Apple IIgs Serial Port driver
    10 - Single Speed SSC driver
    11 - Multiple Spd SSC driver (IIc port)
    12 - No Carrier SSC driver
   Which? [1-12] _
```

Choices 2-7 are for Internal Modems that require a special driver. If you have one of these modems, select it and press RETURN. Otherwise, select the proper Serial driver and press RETURN.

If you have selected one of the External Drivers, you now need to select a modem type. If you see your modem listed, select it and press RETURN. If it's not listed, try the Generic 'AT' Compatible Modem. See the "Appendices" section for further information.

After selecting the modem type, you are given the chance to change the Initialization String the software sends to your modem. You may want to add an 'M0' to the end of the string to turn off the modems speaker. In most cases, pressing RETURN for the defaults is fine.

Next, you can change the Answer String. This is the string that will be sent to the modem to answer an incoming call. Again, in most cases the default works for most applications.

After the answer string you need to select a type of Carrier Detection. If you have a serial interface that supports carrier detect correctly, (Apple SSC does not) then you may use a straight cable and choose Option 2. Otherwise, use the appropriate null modem cable (see the "Internet Setup Guide" for specifications). Once you have your null modem cable connected, choose Option 1.

Finally, choose the appropriate slot for your modem and the speed it should be initialized at. Typically this is the same as the highest speed the modem supports.

Printer and Clock

Once you have selected your modem, you will have to tell the
system what kind of printer interface card you have. If you have no
printer, then select the "No Printer In System" option, and you will be
taken to the clock configuration. If you do have a printer, you will be
asked to enter the slot which contains the printer interface card.

```
                - Printer Interfaces -

     1 - Apple //c built-in port
     2 - Apple Super Serial Card (SSC)
     3 - Apple IIgs built-in port
     4 - Generic Printer Driver
     5 - Star Micronics Grafstar
     6 - Orange Micro Grappler card
     7 - Apple Parallel interface
     8 - Epson APL printer card
     9 - Appricorn Parallel card
    10 - Tyvec Printer Interface
    11 - No Printer in system
Which? [1-11] _
```

GBBS Pro will then ask you what kind of clock you have. If you
do not have a clock, select Option 11 "No Clock In System". If you
have selected a clock that needs a slot, you will be asked to enter the
slot number it resides in. *GBBS* can display the time in 12-hour or
24-hour (military) time, as presented on the next screen. Choose one
and press RETURN.

```
                - Reconfigure Clock -

     1 - Thunderclock Compatible
     2 - A.E. Timemaster II H.O.
     3 - A.E. Serial Pro
     4 - A.E. Ultra Clock
     5 - A.E. //c System Clock
     6 - SMT No-Slot Clock
     7 - ProDOS Compatible Clock
     8 - Mountain Hardware Clock
     9 - Prometheus Versacard
    10 - IIgs Built-in Clock
    11 - No Clock in System
Which? [1-11] _
```

Mass Storage Device

Finally, you need to specify where to install your *GBBS Pro* system. A minimum of 512 KB free is required on your mass storage device. This can be a hard disk, 3.5" 800 KB floppy disk, or another storage device. *GBBS Pro* considers any storage device with more than 512 KB to be a mass storage device.

GBBS Pro will ask you for the Slot and Drive number of your mass storage device. If the media is removable it must be formatted ahead of time. It will then check to see that you have sufficient space available. The program will create a subdirectory called "GBBS. PRO". Once GBBS has all the needed information, it will copy BBS System files onto the mass storage device.

The last version of *GBBS Pro* that can run from 5.25" floppy disks is 1.3j. If you choose to use floppy storage and version 1.3j or older, *GBBS* will ask you how many disk drives you have. You will be told to remove the Configuration Diskette from the drive and insert a few blank disks that *GBBS* will format. After it is finished formatting these disks, it will ready itself to copy files. First it will ask you to insert a formatted disk, and then will copy files onto the disks. After each disk is finished, you will be told what to label it, and will be prompted to enter a new disk until each formatted disk is processed.

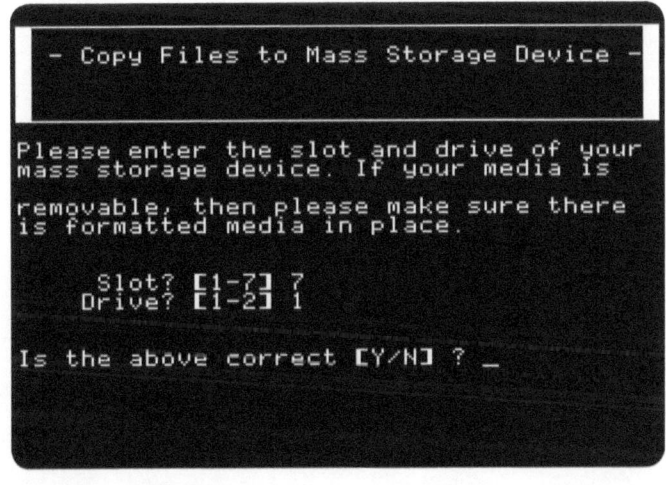

Starting *GBBS Pro*

Once copying of the files has completed, your system is configured and ready to run. It says, "Boot up your mass storage device and type 'PREFIX GBBS.PRO/PROGRAM'. Type '-ACOS' to start your system."

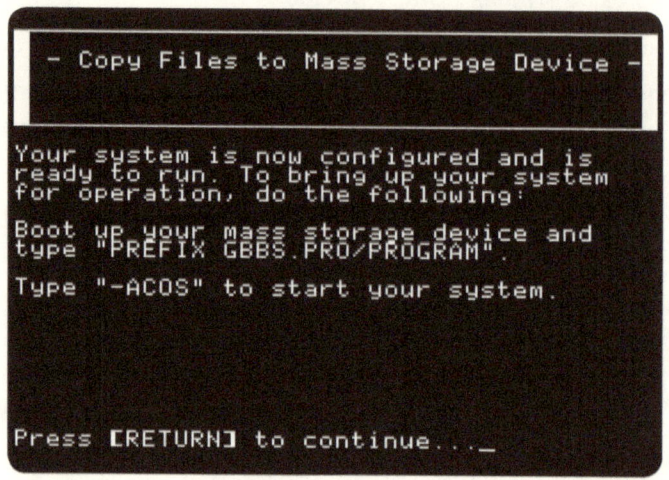

You will be asked to press RETURN and your computer will reboot. You can now start your *GBBS Pro* BBS.

Making a Bootable Volume

It is advantageous to make your *GBBS* volume bootable. Otherwise, you will need to boot into ProDOS first, and then redirect your ProDOS prefix to the GBBS.PRO/PROGRAM directory every time you restart your computer.

The Apple IIe Enhanced, Apple IIc ROM-3 / ROM-4, IIc Plus, and IIGS have the ability to boot from an Apple 3.5" drive using the PR#5 command.

ProDOS 2.03 is the last version from Apple. Using the latest version of ProDOS is recommended – currently ProDOS 2.4.2 by John Brooks. ProDOS 2.4.2 includes the program launcher Bitsy-Bye that is a very convenient way to launch *GBBS* from your mass storage volume. The ProDOS 2.4.2 disk image also includes *Copy II Plus*.

Using a copy utility, create a subdirectory on the root of your mass storage volume called "CONFIG". Using the GBBS.CONFIG disk as the source, copy the file "CONFIG.SYSTEM" into the subdirectory "CONFIG". Then copy the "PRODOS" file from the 2.4.2 system disk onto the root of your mass storage volume.

When you boot from your mass storage volume or 800K diskette, you can use the Bitsy-Bye launcher to point to your GBBS.PRO volume to run "ACOS", or you can point to the CONFIG volume to run "CONFIG.SYSTEM" in order to make configuration changes to your BBS.

Happy BBS-ing.

Internet Setup Guide

by Gene Buckle

This is a basic tutorial for setting up an Internet-connected BBS using *GBBS Pro* and a real or emulated Apple IIe or IIGS computer.

In order to connect your real or virtual Apple IIe to the Internet, you're going to need to set up a "modem emulator." There's a number of different choices out there, but this tutorial covers "tcpser." What *tcpser* does is act as a bridge between the Internet and your Apple II, or other vintage computer. As far as your Apple II is concerned, it's talking to a real modem.

Setting up a host for *tcpser* is pretty simple. Note that *tcpser* can be built for Linux, Windows, and pretty much any BSD-derived operating system (OpenBSD, FreeBSD, NetBSD, Darwin, etc.) This tutorial covers two methods. The first is a Raspberry Pi / Linux configuration and the second is a Windows configuration.

Linux / Raspberry Pi or Windows

For the Raspberry Pi method, you'll need the following items:

- Raspberry Pi 3

- USB to Serial adapter – units that use the Prolific PL-2303 chipset are preferred and are known to work well. Good examples include adapters from Sabrent and TRENDnet.

- Powered USB 2.0 hub – The Raspberry Pi cannot provide the power that the USB to Serial adapter needs, so it has to be plugged into the hub. The advantage is that the Raspberry Pi can be powered from the hub as well.

- Null Modem cable – This is a special serial cable that is used to connect your Apple II to the USB to Serial adapter.

- *tcpser* software.

If you're using a PC as the host, the Raspberry Pi and the USB hub are not needed.

Null Modem Cable

In order to connect your Apple II to the host running *tcpser*, a Null Modem cable is needed. This is a special cable that is designed to allow two computers to communicate over a serial link. This cable is needed because the connection on both the host serial end and Apple II end is known as DTE (Data Terminal Equipment). When trying to get a serial link going DTE to DTE, some wires have to be swapped in the cable. This is not the case when going from a DTE device, to a DCE (Data Communication Equipment) device like a modem.

The serial connector on the Apple II is typically a 25-pin connector and the connector on the computer or Raspberry Pi end is often a 9-pin connector. The chart shows how the wires are connected between the two to make a Null Modem cable if you want to make your own:

DE9 to DB25 Null Modem Cable			
DE-9 Pin #	Name	Name	DB-25 Pin #
8	CTS	RTS	4
7	RTS	CTS	5
3	TXD	RXD	3
2	RXD	TXD	2
4	DTR	DCD	8
1	DCD	DTR	20
5	GND	GND	7

Cables of this type are easily found online. One example is the StarTech CNM925FM. Make sure that the cable is a "full" Null Modem cable with a pinout that matches the chart, otherwise it may not work properly.

Super Serial Card Configuration

On the Apple II side, setup the Super Serial Card like this:

Set the jumper block with the triangle on it so that the tip of the triangle points toward "MODEM."

SW1 is the first switch block, SW2 is the second. Set Switches to:

SW1 switches 1-4: Off On Off On for 2400 baud
SW1-5 and SW1-6: On for "Communications Mode"
SW2-1: On for 1 stop bit
SW2-2: On for 8 bits
SW2-4: On for no parity
SW2-6: On to enable interrupts (Off for Apple II or II Plus)

tcpser for Linux / Raspberry Pi

In order to get *tcpser* installed on your Raspberry Pi, you need the source code from the Git repository where it lives. If you don't have Git or the C compiler installed on your Raspberry Pi, those need to be installed first – please search the Internet if you need help.

Obtaining the source code for *tcpser* is very simple – simply "clone" into the Git repository where it's stored. The Git repository to clone into is: https://github.com/FozzTexx/tcpser

The command to obtain the software is:
```
git clone https://github.com/FozzTexx/tcpser
```

At the beginning of the process you'll see "Cloning into 'tcpser'." Once the clone is finished, change to the *tcpser* directory and type "make" to compile the program. When the compile finishes, you're ready to go!

tcpser for Windows

If using Windows for your *tcpser* host, a pre-compiled binary is available at: https://gbbs.applearchives.com.

The zip file contains the "tcpser.exe" program as well as two DLLs that are required for it to function. Please put the DLLs in the same directory that tcpser.exe is in, otherwise the program may not work.

Running *tcpser* for Your BBS

You need to identify what serial device you want *tcpser* to talk to while it's running. On a Raspberry Pi with a single USB serial adapter, it will be called "/dev/ttyUSB0". On a Windows system with a serial port at COM1, it will be called "/dev/ttyS0". Serial ports referenced by *tcpser* are counted from zero on Windows, so /dev/ttyS1 corresponds to COM2, /dev/ttyS2 corresponds to COM3, etc.

Decide what Telnet port you want *tcpser* to watch for connections. Port 23 is the standard Telnet port, but using something like 2300 or 6502 is recommended. The reason is that if your BBS is on a non-standard port, it will prevent port scanners from disturbing your BBS.

Choose a baud rate for your BBS that's the fastest that your BBS software can reliably support. With *GBBS Pro* 1.3 and earlier, the driver appears to only support up to 2400 baud. This is unsurprising considering the modems average users had available to them in 1986. *GBBS Pro* 2.2 (and possibly others after 1.3j) support baud rates up to 38,400. Because *tcpser* runs at a fixed baud rate, you need to configure the BBS to run at the rate you've chosen for *tcpser*. If you notice characters are being dropped at 38,400, slow it down and test again.

Available baud rates for *tcpser* are: 300, 1200, 2400, 4800, 9600, 19200, 38400, 57600, and 115200.

Create a short text file that will be sent to a caller when they try to connect and someone is already on the BBS. This is known as the "busy" file and should let the user know that the system is busy and that they should try connecting again at a later time.

Once *tcpser* is built or downloaded, you can run it with the following options:

```
tcpser -d /dev/ttyUSB0 -s 2400 -p 2300 -B busy-msg.txt
-i "X3S0=1&C1&D2S2=128"
```

`-d /dev/ttyUSB0` — What device *tcpser will* use.
`-s 2400`   — Set the port baud rate to 2400.
`-p 2300`   — Listen on port 2300 for incoming connections.
`-B busy-msg.txt` — Defines the name of the "busy file."

`-i "X3S0=1&C1&D2S2=128"` — Configures *tcpser's* virtual modem:

      `X3`   — Enable busy signal detection.
      `S0=1`   — Set to auto answer.
      `&C1`   — Enable DCD after carrier detected.
      `&D2`   — Dropping DTR causes connection to be closed.
      `S2=128` — Sets modem "escape" character to ASCII 128.

On the *GBBS* side, configure the system for a Hayes 2400 baud modem. If your version of *GBBS* supports baud rates higher than 2400, there's no reason you can't use those higher rates with *tcpser*. Just specify that faster rate the same way you did with 2400 baud.

The simplest way to run *tcpser* is via a script (Linux/Unix) or batch file (Windows). These examples assume the first serial port, 2400 baud, and port 2300:

Linux:
```
/path/to/tcpser -d /dev/ttyUSB0 -s 2400 -p 2300
-B busy-msg.txt -i "X3S0=1&C1&D2S2=128"
```

Windows:
```
X:\path\to\tcpser -d /dev/ttyS0 -s 2400 -p 2300
-B busy-msg.txt -i "X3S0=1&C1&D2S2=128"
```

Save the relevant command line to a file, "runbbs.sh" for Linux or "runbbs.bat" for Windows – there's your script or batch file! Keep in mind that under Linux, the script needs to be started with "sudo" so *tcpser* has permission to access the serial device on your system. For example: `sudo runbbs.sh`

In Linux, you need to mark the script as executable by issuing "`chmod script-name.sh +x`". This is not necessary in Windows.

That's pretty much all there is to it! Just configure your BBS as you normally would, hook it up to your host via a Null Modem cable and go!

CHAPTER 3

Running the System & Commands

Running the Software

First, boot into ProDOS and run BASIC.SYSTEM. Then type "PREFIX GBBS.PRO/PROGRAM" and RETURN then type "-ACOS" and RETURN. You will see an inverse window with the heading "ACOS LOADER V:2.2" on it. This is the program that actually runs the bulletin board. At the bottom of the screen will be the message "SOURCE MODULE [LOGON.SEG]:". Press RETURN to start the system running.

Once the system starts to run, the screen will go blank and you will get the message "One moment, compiling segment...." Finally, a title screen will appear with the name of your system on the screen. You will also see a little block in the upper right corner of your screen. You will notice that the block is constantly changing. This indicates that the system is running and waiting for a call.

If you are using *GBBS Pro* version 1.3j or earlier:

2 or 3 Drives: Insert the disk labeled "BOOT" and turn on your computer. The inverse screen labeled "BOOT LOADER V: 2.2" will appear. Next, insert the disk called "SYSTEM" into your second drive and press RETURN. You will get the message "CHECKING FILES...", told where to place each of your disks, and asked to press RETURN to start your system running.

4 Drives: Insert the disk named "BOOT" and turn on your computer. The inverse screen labeled "ACOS LOADER V: 2.2" will appear. Next, insert the disk called "SYSTEM" into your 2nd drive, the disk called "BULLETINS" into your 3rd drive, and the disk called "MAIL" into your 4th drive. Press RETURN and the system will start running.

Logging on the System

You are now ready to log in for the first time. To do this, press the "G" key. The system will now switch into the local mode and will begin operation. The screen will clear and ask you how you would like to logon to the system. You want to automatically log on so type "Y" or "1". The system will proceed to automatically log you in.

You will now be placed at the main command menu, and the screen will display the main system prompt: **(::)(Main Level Option (?=Help):**

```
#1    STEVE WOZNIAK of SEATTLE, WA      Stats: CT=0  CM=0   UP=0  DL=0   BP=0
Ph: 206-000-0000 00/00/00   1-######## Flg: 11111111111111111111111111111111111

:::::::::::::::::::::::::::::::::::::::::::::::::::::::::::::::::::::::
:                  List of Supported Commands                      :
:::::::::::::::::::::::::::::::::::::::::::::::::::::::::::::::::::::::
:                 <<B>> Goto the Bulletin Boards                   :
:::::::::::::::::::::::::::::::::::::::::::::::::::::::::::::::::::::::
: R -> Read mail sent to you        : E -> Examine your system status  :
: S -> Send mail to another user    : F -> Feedback to the Sysop       :
: G -> General files menu           : H -> See the detailed help file  :
: $ -> Read the latest System News  : O -> Other  BBS numbers          :
: I -> Read System Information      : T -> Terminate connection (Logoff) :
: C -> Chat With the Sysop          : U -> See list of users on system :
:::::::::::::::::::::::::::::::::::::::::::::::::::::::::::::::::::::::
: Q -> Quick scan of bulletin boards : D -> Define  system display  parms :
: P -> Change / Update your password : V -> Vote on your  computer equipt :
: L -> Log of todays callers         : X -> Goto the file  transfer  area :
:::::::::::::::::::::::::::::::::::::::::::::::::::::::::::::::::::::::
[::][Main Level] Option (?=Help):_
```

From here, you might want to view the various options that you have on the system. To do this, type "?". The system will now display the Main Menu. This menu contains all the valid commands that a user can type on your system. Of course, you may wish to customize this as you add your own features or sub-boards.

Next, you should go to your main bulletin board and post a message. To do this, type "B". Normally, you would now be placed into the Bulletin Sub-Section. However, since there are no bulletins yet, the system will ask you if you wish to post one. Type "Y" and then enter the subject of your bulletin and to whom.

Now the system will ask you who the message is from (please note that this question is asked to the system operator only, and not to a regular user). You may enter any name you wish, or you may press RETURN to have the system put your name in for you.

You will now be placed in the editor where you can type the text of your bulletin. You may enter up to 4K of text, which is approximately 4,000 characters. When you are finished typing your message, type "/EX" at the beginning of a new line. This tells the system that you are through typing your text.

You will now see a prompt that reads **Option (?=Help):**. Normally, this would be the point that you would wish to edit certain lines. However, if you are content with your message, type "O" which stands for "(O)k". The system will now save your message to disk. If you do not wish to save this message, but rather type a different one, press "N" which stands for (N)ew. The system will ask you if you really wish to type a new message. If so, type "Y". Otherwise, press "N" and you will be taken back to the **Option (?=Help):** prompt.

Once you have posted your message, you will be placed back into the Bulletin Sub-Section. This section deals only with the bulletin board section itself. From here, you may do several things such as reading, posting, or searching for bulletins. If you wish to read the bulletin you just left, type "1", and press RETURN. The system will now display the message. Press "A" to (A)bort back to the main command level.

You should now be back at the **Command (?=Help):** prompt. Once again, you may wish to check the menu to see what you can do (to do this, type "?"). Once you have tried out a few other commands, type "T" to (T)erminate this session and log off your board.

Running Your System

Your board is now ready for the public. However, there are a few things which you must do to maintain your system. Be sure to log on every so often to perform some "housekeeping" duties.

Every time you log on to your system, you will be told one or more of the following:

```
There Are New Bulletins
There Are New Users
You Have Mail Waiting
```

If you do have mail waiting, the system will ask you if you wish to read it now. It is generally a good idea to read through your mail when you first get on the system. As Sysop, you do get a lot of mail and it does pile up.

Next, if you do have new users, you should go to the system section and verify them. Again, it is generally a good idea to verify your users as soon as possible because the Request File does take up a lot of disk space. Also, while you are in the system section, it may be wise to check your log and delete it once you have read it.

Again, the log tends to eat up disk space especially when it is neglected. If you do not want to maintain your Log, there is a way to remove it in the "Modifications" section of this manual.

Finally, you might want to read all the new messages that are on your system simply to keep up with what is going on.

Idletime Commands

The first few commands are those that can be issued while the system is standing idle (that is, when it is waiting for a call). Obviously these are available only on the *GBBS Pro* console itself and there is no menu. These commands maybe entered simply by pressing the appropriate key:

G: **GET ON** – Allows you, the Sysop, to log on the system locally (from your own computer). Upon issuing this command, the computer will beep and you will be asked if you wish to be automatically logged on. If you reply "Yes" to this question, you will automatically be placed into your system. If you reply "No", you will have to follow the same log on procedure as a normal user.

A: **AUTO CONNECT** – Attempt to connect a caller should the modem not be connected at the time the call was originated. When you press the "A" key, *GBBS Pro* will bring your modem off-hook and attempt to make a connection by sending out a carrier.

Q: **QUIT** – Terminate the execution of *GBBS Pro*, and places you into the " *** Restart: S,M,Q ? " prompt. "S" stands for source and will restart the system using the startup module specified at boot time. "M" stands for memory and will restart the segment currently in memory. "Q" will call the ProDOS quit code. **NOTE:** Using "M" can be very dangerous. It is advised that you do not logoff the system after using the "M" option. Press CTRL-RESET and use "S".

Runtime Commands

The following commands can be executed during any time
that the bulletin board is actually being used. These commands are
Control Functions. You must press and hold down the CTRL key
while pressing the appropriate letter key. These functions can only be
performed by the Sysop on the system console.

Ctrl-A   Place you in Chat Mode where you and the user can type
to each other without any interference. To exit Chat Mode,
type "Ctrl-A" again.

Ctrl-R   For those Sysops who can only support forty columns,
pressing "Ctrl-R" will change the top of the screen display
so you may get a listing of the user's stats. When the user
first logs on, the top of the screen will show statistics such
as the number of messages a user has left. Pressing "Ctrl-R"
again will change the display to show the users flag/bit
status. "1" indicates that the flag is set, and "0" indicates
that the flag is not set. Pressing "Ctrl-R" again will cause
the screen display to change. This time displaying such
information as the user's phone number, password, etc.
Pressing "Ctrl-R" a final time will change the display back to
the original screen display.

Ctrl-L   Pressing "Ctrl-L" at any time while a user is on will
automatically log the user off for you.

Ctrl-O   Change the status of the special "Sysop Window" that
appears on the bottom of the screen. After the first time
you press "Ctrl-O", the window will open up on the bottom
and *GBBS Pro* will display "INP:" followed by a blank line.
You will now be able to view all the characters the user is
sending your system. Control characters are proceeded by
a carat (^). If you press "Ctrl-O" again, you will be taken
into the program trace mode. The window will now display
"PRG:". *GBBS Pro* will now display the program statements
as they are executed.

Pressing "Ctrl-Z" during the Program Trace Mode will cause the program to execute itself one statement at a time. Typing any key other than "Ctrl-Z" will resume normal program execution. Pressing "Ctrl-O" again will close the Sysop Window.

Ctrl-P   Dump the current screen display to your printer (if you have one).

Ctrl-V   Place you in the executive mode. The user is told to wait and *GBBS Pro* will switch into local mode so you may perform any Sysop function. Pressing "Ctrl-V" again will restore control to the user. Remember, the user will have control whenever you leave them. Before putting the user back online, make sure that you (A)bort from the System.

Ctrl-^   Clear the contents of the 128 character type-ahead buffer.

Ctrl-]   Hide or display a user's password. By default, a user's password will not be displayed. Pressing "Ctrl-)" once will uncover the user's password with asterisks. Pressing it again will cause the password to be hidden.

System Commands

The following is a list of each command and its use on your system after you have configured your program. This is very similar to what your users will see when they type "H" for Help. In each section of the board there is context sensitive help.

B: Access to the Main Bulletin Board on the system – the command "J" (for jump) does the same thing. From here you can type "?" to see a list of commands and get more help. You also can access all of the other bulletin boards on the system from this point.

B#:   Access directly to that Bulletin Board from the system as long as it exists and you have access to it. (i.e. "B6" puts you on Board 6). The command "J#" (for jump) does the same thing.

C: Chat with the Sysop. You need only issue this command once as the Sysop is constantly reminded that someone wishes to chat.

Chatting
with a user

D: Define your system display parameters with a menu to edit them:

    B: Defines the type of backspace mode the editor should use for your terminal program. If you see three numbers you have a destructible backspace. Six numbers show you have a non-destructible backspace.

    N: By changing the "Nulls" value, you can change the amount of time *GBBS Pro* will pause after each RETURN.

    P: Sets the Auto-page mode. If it is on, there will be a pause after 20 lines. Pressing RETURN will display the next 20 lines. Pressing the SPACEBAR will abort from reading the entire file.

    Q: Quit display parameters.

    S: Toggle on/off the viewing of your phone number to other users on the system.

    V: Video Width can be changed from the default of 40 to 32, 64, or 80 columns wide.

E: The system contains a list of stats on each user as well as general system stats. These include your user number, the last date you called, part of your security level, the last caller, the number of calls the system has received today, your logon time, the present time, how long you have been connected, how much time is left if there is a system time limit, and all of the different levels you have access to.

F: Send comments directly to the Sysop using "Feedback". You will use the editor to create your message. The Sysop will be able to reply to your feedback.

G: List of "General" files. Each number listed represents a different topic. Enter the number you wish to look at or RETURN when done. Not available to guests.

H: Typing "H" is context sensitive and will give you help in different areas of the system. There is a help file for the Bulletin Board. The "Transfer" system which contains Download / Upload, and the editor. The file is called "SYS.HELP".

I: List "Information" about the system such as which *GBBS* software you are using, hardware configuration, and system sponsor. You can modify the "SYS.INFO" file to change the information.

J: Jump. See the command "B".

J#: Jump. See the command "B#".

L: Shows the caller log for the day. It is deleted automatically as the system does its day change operations. Not available to guests.

O: List of other *GBBS* bulletin board telephone numbers. Not available to guests.

P: New users who logged on as one-time guests can change their mind and can use this command to obtain a Password. If you are a verified user, you can use this command to change your password to 4-8 characters. Your user number remains the same.

Q: Global Quickscan with optional beginning board #.

Reading
Mail

R: Display your mail (if you have any waiting). After each letter, you will have the following options:

  A: Auto-Reply to a letter. Allow you to reply to the person who has written you.

  C: Continue. Display the next letter that you have, if there is one. Other methods of continuing are "N" and "ENTER".

  F: Forward a letter. Send a copy of the letter to whomever you wish. You must specify the receiver with either their name or user number.

  P: Print mail to printer. Sysop only.

  Q: Force the program to stop retrieving mail.

  R: Reread the letter. Re-display the letter you just read.

  W: Write a letter to disk as a standard text file. You will first be asked to enter the name of the text file that will be written. GBBS will then write the contents of the letter to this text file. Sysop only.

S: Send Electronic Mail. When you first type "S" the system will ask "To whom (#,B,<CR>):". At this point, you may send a single letter by typing the user's name or user's number that you wish to send mail to. The "B" command will allow you to do a "Bulk Mailing". That is, send many copies of the same letter to different users without having to retype it each time. The first time you press "B" you will be asked to whom you wish to send a copy. You will then be prompted to enter the letter that you wish to do a bulk mailing with. After you enter the letter for the first time, you again will be asked to whom you wish to send a copy. From this point until you exit the E-Mail section, the letter does not need to be retyped but will automatically be sent. Not available to guests.

T: Terminate your connection from the system. Your mail will be deleted and your stats updated. The system keeps track of how many times you call in a day, the total number of calls made to the system, how many uploads you've made, the number of downloads you've taken, and the number of bulletins you've posted.

U: List of all or some of the system "Users". You can search for one name, a partial name, everyone with the same first and last name, or get the entire list with RETURN. Next to each user's name will be a number that should be used for sending mail. Typing "?" will give you more help. Not available to guests.

V: Voting system. Not available to guests.

X: Download or Upload programs from the system. After you choose the program you want to download, you have a choice to use "ASCII" or "Xmodem" download or "Exit". If you continue, press RETURN to begin the download. Xmodem download requires that your terminal program have the capabilities to use this feature. You will need to use a terminal program with a capture buffer such as *ASCII Express Pro* or *ProTerm*. After you save it, capture it to disk and "EXEC" the file:

> **H**:   Help for file transfers.
>
> **L**:   List available files.
>
> **Q**:   Quit transfer system.
>
> **U**:   Upload a file:
> > **A**: ASCII
> > **D**: DOS Xmodem
> > **P**: ProDOS Xmodem
> > **S**: Standard Xmodem
>
> **#**:   Download file #:
> > **A**: ASCII
> > **D**: DOS Xmodem
> > **P**: ProDOS Xmodem
> > **S**: Standard Xmodem

$:   Display the most recent system news.

?:   List of available commands almost any place in the system.

%:   Puts you into a section that is called SYSTEM (a section for the Sysop only) that allows you to run your system.

Bulletin Commands

The following commands pertain to the *GBBS Pro* bulletin sub-section. To get to these commands, type "B" at the main prompt:

(xx)(Main Level) Option (?=Help):

(xx)(Board # 1-##) Option (?=Help):

The Option Menu Bar tells you what board you are presently on and how many bulletins are posted. From here you can type a question mark to see the following list of commands:

>:   Next board.

<:   Previous board.

/:   Short help.

?:   Short help.

#:   Enter the number of a bulletin on a board and start a forward retrieval from that bulletin.

A: Abort (quit).

B: The "Browse" command lets you look for certain bulletins. When you select this command, you are first asked for a search string. You will next be asked if you wish to "Mark" bulletins for later retrieval. After answering this question, *GBBS Pro* will search the titles of each message on that board and display each title that contains the search string. Please note that *GBBS Pro* can and will find the search string even if it appears inside a word. If you selected to "Mark" your bulletins, the ones you have selected for retrieval will be displayed.

F: List all the bulletins starting "Forward" at a certain number.

G: Force the system to do a "Global Quickscan" which will scan each board on your system and look for new messages. If there are new messages on a board, you will be asked if you want to read them. Skip them, or quit from Global Quickscan.

H: Show help file.

J#:   Jump to another board [board #].

K: "Kills" bulletins you have left. The user will only be able to kill the bulletins that they have left. You as the Sysop will be able to kill any user's bulletins.

L: List boards.

M: When you "Scan" or "Browse" the subjects, you will be asked if you want to "Allow marking?" of the messages to read them after you choose them with a "Yes / No / Quit" option. After you have finished reading the marked messages the first time, "M" will display the same marked messages again.

N: Retrieves "New" bulletins that have been left since the last time you called.

P: "Post" a bulletin for all users to see. You will be placed into the editor to enter your message.

Q: Quit.

R#:   Sequential Retrieval – Reverse [from message #].

S: "Scans" message subjects starting at a certain number. If you wish to "Mark Messages" after each title, you should answer "Y". This will allow you to read the bulletins you "marked" when you are done seeing the titles. After 15 bulletin titles are displayed, you will be asked if you wish to see more. If you have been on the system before, you will see a " * " in front of the number of the titles you have not yet read.

T: Terminate Connection.

Bulletin Bar Commands

After reading a bulletin using the N)ew, F)orward, or M)arked retrieval, a line of text will appear that says: **(Bx #1 of y) ? or cmd (N)#**. There are several functions that can be accessed from this "bar" of commands:

+:   Tell *GBBS Pro* that you no longer wish the "(Bx #1 of y) ? or cmd (N)#" prompt to be displayed between bulletins. After pressing "+", the system will no longer display the command bar but instead display all the bulletins on that sub-board.

<CR>: Done reading, return to main menu via the RETURN key.

?:   Show command list.

A: Reply to a bulletin. After typing this command you will first be asked if the reply is a private letter. If it is, then the message will be sent through E-Mail. If you indicated that this message was not private, it will automatically be posted as if you were leaving a bulletin. The subject of this new bulletin will be the same as the one you are replying to.

D: Dump (appears to leave message system).

E: Available to Sysops or privileged users only (users which have "flag(2)" of their security level set to 1). Pressing "E" will load the bulletin that was just displayed into memory and allow you to edit it. For privileged users, this command will only work if the bulletin belongs to them.

K: Remove the bulletin that was last displayed from the sub board that you are in. This command will work for any user as long as the message belonged to them. A Sysop can remove a bulletin that belongs to anyone.

M: Reply to message.

N: Display the next bulletin, if there is one.

P: Print message. Sysop only.

Q: Force the system to stop retrieving bulletins and will take you to the "Option (?=Help):" prompt so that you may perform other bulletin functions.

R: Re-display the last bulletin that was shown.

S: Move message to another board. Sysop only.

W: Write the bulletin to disk as a text file. Pressing "W" will prompt to specify a filename. *GBBS Pro* will then write the contents of the bulletin into a text file with the name specified.

X: Download message by Xmodem.

Editor Commands

The following commands are used in the first column of each line within the editor as you are typing in your text. Both " . " and " / " are valid to start the command. NOTE: They will not work in the middle of your text.

Text Dot Commands

.A   Automatically abort your text entry. Before it clears the editor it will first ask you if you wish to abort.

.D   Delete a line or range of lines. It must be followed by a line number (".D6" to delete line 6) or a range of lines (".D5,7" to delete lines 5 thru 7).

.DL   Delete the last line of text you have entered. If the editor is empty, this command has no effect.

.E   Edit a line of text. The command must be followed by the line number of the line you wish to edit (".E6" to edit line 6).

.EL   Edit the last line of text that you entered. If the editor is empty, it will have no effect.

.H   Print out the Dot command help file on the screen and let you continue to write your message.

.I   Insert a line or lines of text anywhere within a message. The command must be followed by a line number (".I6" to insert before line 6). Once you have finished inserting text you must type "DONE" to leave the insert mode.

.L   List the contents of the editor to your screen. By adding a line number or range of lines, you can list one or several lines of your message.

.LL   List the last line of text that you entered. It is most useful from remote when you have a noisy phone line and wish to make sure the line you typed made it to the system without any problems.

.LY   The same as the ".L" command, except that the line numbers that go along with the text will also be listed.

.N   Clear the contents of the editor and enter new text. The system will ask you if you really wish to enter a new message.

.O   Save the file without allowing you to edit the file again. This is helpful if you have typed in the file before you called this system and only want to upload your file.

.P   Toggle prompt.

.S   Save your message to disk. It is the same as the ".O" command.

.Z   Show editor bytes used.

Editor Control Commands

These commands are used in the editor. Press CTRL plus the appropriate letter key at the same time. If the user has non-destructible backspacing (your terminal program will not erase a character when it backs over it), some of these commands may not work:

Ctrl-B: Move the cursor to the beginning of the current line of text that you are typing.

Ctrl-C: Center the current line of text that you are typing.

Ctrl-D: Delete the character that is directly after the blinking cursor and shift all text after the cursor one space to the left.

Ctrl-E: Move the cursor to the end of the current line of text that you are typing.

Ctrl-F: Insert a space directly after the cursor and shift all text after the cursor one space to the right.

Ctrl-I: Tab the cursor by printing eight spaces. The TAB key does the same thing.

Ctrl-L: Move cursor to last word.

Ctrl-N: Move cursor to next word.

Ctrl-Q: Make the cursor to move back one word. It does nothing at the beginning of a line.

Ctrl-T: Delete all the text from the cursor to the end of the current line of text that you are typing.

Ctrl-U: The forward character command. It is the same as pressing the forward arrow key on the Apple keyboard. It will move the cursor forward one character.

Ctrl-W: Make the cursor to move forward one word. It does nothing at the end of the line.

Ctrl-X: Delete the entire line that you are currently typing.

Edit Commands

These commands can be entered at the "**Option (?=Help):**" prompt:

A: "Abort" the message and exit the editor.

C: "Continue" will re-enter the editor. All new text will be appended to the end of the message.

D: By entering a line number you can "Delete" one or more lines. Enter RETURN to abort. Enter an "L" to list the message prior to deleting.

E: "Edit" a line of the message by entering its line number and re-typing that line. Entering "L" will list the message as above, but line numbers will be shown before each line of text.

I: "Insert" line(s) of text before the line number you specify. You can enter "L" to list the message with line numbers.

L: "List" the message in part or in whole. Enter a starting line number or RETURN to list the entire message. If a starting line was entered, enter the ending line number or RETURN to list through the end of the message.

N: Erase the current message and start over.

O: "Ok". The message is complete and ready to save.

R: "Read" an external file. It is only available to Sysops. After pressing "R", specify the file name. The system will load the file into memory and return back to the option prompt. NOTE: This command will only read the first 4K of your text file.

S: This command is the same as "O". It indicates your message is complete and ready to save.

W: "Write" the contents of the editor to a disk file. After pressing "W", specify the filename.

Z: Show editor bytes used.

Sysop Commands

A: ABORTs you back to the main command level.

D: Execute a ProDOS command. The following commands are
supported. NOTE: Only the first letter of the command needs to
be entered:

CATALOG (drive specifier:) – Display the files on the
specified drive. If a drive specifier is not used, the current logged
drive will be used. You cannot use a ProDOS pathname. Using
"CATALOG B:" would display the files in the system directory.

RENAME (drive specifier:) name1,name2 – Rename a file
on the specified drive. If a drive specifier is not used, the current
logged drive will be used. If name1 is not found on the specified
drive, you will get an error.

DELETE (drive specifier:) name1 – Erase a file from the
specified drive. If a drive specifier is not given, the current drive
will be used. If name1 could not be found on the specified drive,
you will get an error.

LOCK (drive specifier:) name1 – Lock a file on the specified
drive so that it may not be deleted or renamed. If name1 could
not be found, you will get an error.

UNLOCK (drive specifier:) name1 – Unlock a file on the
specified drive so that it may be deleted or renamed. If name1
could not be found, you will get an error.

TYPE (drive specifier:) name1.type – Change the file type of
the file. If a drive specifier is not given, the current drive is used.
The file type is given in letter form. (i.e. BIN,TXT).

XATALOG (drive specifier:) – This command is the same as
CATALOG except it is shown in 80-column format. It is just
like a ProDOS CATALOG – all information is given.

F: Display any text file. Specify the name of the file in the following format: (drive specifier:) name1. If you do not use a drive specifier the current drive is used.

G: Get a text file into the *GBBS Pro* editor. Simply specify the name of the file to load in the form: **(drive specifier:) name1**. The file will be loaded from the current drive if no drive specifier is given.

K: Delete a user. Specify the number of the user to delete. Confirmation will be requested before the user is deleted.

Disowning a user

L: View the caller log. When you press "L" you have these options:

   D: Delete the caller log. Don't neglect to delete the log periodically as it takes up valuable space.

   P: Dump the contents of the caller log to the printer.

Q: Quit the log functions and return to System level prompt.

S: Show the contents of the caller log to the screen.

N: Add a new user to the system without the user logging on. This command does not check for duplicate names.

P: Edit the PASSWORD or other user stats. Enter the number of the user to edit and their stats will appear, each preceded by a letter. If you wish to edit the user who is currently on the system, type "C" instead of a user number.

   A: Change the name of the user.

   B: Edit the place from which the user is calling from. The length of the user's name plus the length of where the are calling from may not exceed 28 characters.

   C: Change the user's password. The new password may be from 1 to 8 characters long. When you are typing in the new password, you need not type the user's number.

   D: Change the user's phone status. When typing the phone number, the presence of a hyphen between the area code and the number indicates that the number is to be invisible to other users from the Userlist command. That is, 000-000-0000 is invisible to other users while 000 000-0000 is visible. If you change the second '-' to a '#', '%' or an '*' then that changes the status of the user when you use the Userpurge program. The person with a phone number of 000 000#0000 is deleted three months later than others with the same last call date. The user with the number 000 000%0000 is deleted six months later than other users with the some last call date. The user with an '*' in place of the second '-' is never deleted.

   E: Change the user's security status. If you are not familiar with the way the security system works, type "?". This will display each "Access Level" and ask you if you wish to give the user access to this level. You may type "Y" for yes, "N" for no, or "Q" to quit. If you are familiar with the security system and your access levels you may simply type a series of 1s and 0s as a string. Each number from left to right represents a security flag. A "1" indicates that the user has the flag set (i.e. the user has access to that level) while a "0" indicates that the user does not have the flag set (i.e. they do not have access to that level). When typing in the security flags in string form, you need not type all 34 characters.

R: Read one-by-one, the comments received from new users who answered the questions in the "SYS.NEWINFO" file. After reading each comment, you can do one of the following:

    A: Reply to the user via Electronic Mail. Pressing "A" is similar to (A)uto-reply to a letter in E-Mail.

    C: Continue and take you to the next new user request.

    K: Kill (delete) the user and remove the user from the user file.

    Q: Quit reading requests. This command will stop displaying the request file and return you to the System level prompt.

    R: Reread this user's information and display the user's information that was provided during logon.

    V: Verify the user. When pressing "V", the system pulls up the some statistics for the user as the "P" Edit User command. Then edit any characteristic of that user, such as his security status, time limit, etc.

Once you are through editing a user, Pressing RETURN will allow you to do the following:

    A: Abort and do not write the user's statistics back to disk, instead returning to the System level prompt.

R: Return to the editing of a user's stats.

S: Write the user's statistics back to disk. Any changes that
         have been made will be updated. After saving the statistics,
         the program will return to the System level prompt.

S: Change the date if you do not have a clock. The new date should
         be in the form mm/dd/yy. NOTE: If you have a clock, do NOT
         use this command.

T: Terminate connection.

W: Update the news file. Use this command each time you update
         your system news to make sure that each user will see it.

CHAPTER 4

Utility Program Reference

Using the Configuration Program

To run the configuration program, place the GBBS.CONFIG disk into your main disk drive and boot your computer. Answer "N" to the question "Do initial configuration?".

```
   GBBS Config Program - Version 2.2
   Copyright 1986-2017 Kevin Smallwood.

When you do an initial configure, all
previous data will be destroyed and
replaced with the new configuration.
All old data will be lost.

Do you want to do an Initial Configure?
[Y/N] _
```

You will now be asked for the pathname where the file "ACOS. OBJ" resides. Enter the pathname from where you run the bulletin board. Normally, the path will be something like "/HARD1/ GBBS.PRO". If you are using a floppy-based system, place your boot disk into your second drive and enter the pathname (usually "/PROGRAM").

If the drive spins and the configuration program comes back to the same screen again, the program was unable to locate the "ACOS.OBJ" file. Re-check and make sure that you are entering the correct location of your boot disk or mass storage device.

If things went correctly, and configuration located the files that it needs, you will get the main screen with 10 options:

```
  GBBS Config Program - Version 2.2
  Copyright 1986-2017 Kevin Smallwood.

Select an Option:
   1 - Reconfigure Modem
   2 - Reconfigure Video
   3 - Reconfigure Printer
   4 - Reconfigure Clock
   5 - Reconfigure Storage
   6 - Edit Profanity Filter
   7 - Edit Bulletin Board Info
   8 - Sort and Print Userlist
   9 - Purge Users From System
  10 - Exit Configure

Which? [1-10] _
```

Once you are finished using the configuration program, choose Option 10 to quit. Configuration will exit to ProDOS via the "quit code". From there, you can exit to BASIC or run another application including the bulletin board system.

Changing Hardware

Changing the hardware configuration of a system is easy. Once the configuration program has been run and the main command menu is present, select Option 1 through 4 to reconfigure the Modem, Video Console, Printer, or Clock respectively. Once the option has been selected, choose correct hardware and press RETURN. If you make a mistake during this process, you can press ESC at any time to abort back to the previous screen.

Changing Drive Setup

To change the drive allocation and to reassign files to different locations, select Option 5 "Reconfigure Storage" from the main command menu in configuration. A screen will be displayed titled "Drive Allocation" with the letters "A:" to "I:" listed along the left hand side with pathnames following some of them.

The letters "A:" thru "I:" represent certain groups of files used by the bulletin board system. The pathnames represent where these different groups of files are stored. Under ProDOS, the drive specifiers are defined as follows for where items are located:

A: Program Segments
B: System Files
C: General Files
D: Downloads
E: Uploads
F: Bulletins
G: Electronic Mail

The remaining drives "H:" thru "I:" are left open for your expansion. You can change the setting of a drive specifier by entering its letter and pressing RETURN. Enter the new pathname and press RETURN.

Once you change one or more drive specifiers, save the changes back to disk with the "Q" command. You will then need to move the actual files affected by your changes. In the case of the uploads, no files need be moved since the drive specifier is just the location where future uploads will be saved.

However, all the other drive specifiers point to existing data. For example, "C:" points to the general files. If you were to change "C:" to a new location, and not copy the actual general files over there when the system accesses the general files section, it would not find any data. You must move the files accordingly. You can use most any copy program such as *Pro-Copy*, *Cat Doctor*, *Filer*, or *Copy II Plus*.

Editing the Profanity Filter

The system has a profanity filter built into its editor. When a user writes a message (either electronic mail or a bulletin) and saves it, the system will go through the document word by word and replace any offensive text with asterisks (*). While the system comes with a standard list of obscenities, you may need to add some or remove some. A warning – the editor will replace even partial words. If the word "HELL" was in the filter and a user entered "HELLO WORLD", it would be changed to "****O WORLD".

To edit the filter, select Option 6 "Edit Profanity Filter" from the main menu of the configuration program. You will be presented with a lettered list of the obscenities that are currently filtered. Use "A" to add another word to the list, "D" to delete an existing word, or "Q" once your changes are complete. Upon completion, your changes will be saved back to disk.

Manipulating Bulletin Boards

To modify the bulletin boards in any way, select Option 7 "Edit Bulletin Board Info" from the main configuration menu. If using a floppy-based system, place the GBBS.SYSTEM disk into an available drive and press RETURN. The GBBS.CONFIG disk must also be accessible. A list of eight options will appear:

```
           - Edit Bulletin Board Info -


Select an Option:
    1) Clear all previous boards
    2) Add a new bulletin board
    3) Delete a bulletin board
    4) Edit an existing board
    5) Swap two bulletin boards
    6) List all bulletin boards
    7) Create board storage file
    8) Return back to main menu
Enter choice [1-8] ? _
```

To add a bulletin board select Option 2 "Add a New Bulletin Board". You will next be asked for the name of the new board. For the name of a board, we generally recommend using "xxx Board" as the basic form. If you want to add a board for Sysops you would want to call it the "Sysop Board".

You should also try to keep your board name between 15 and 25 characters in length. Of course, these are just guidelines as you make the ultimate decision.

You will be presented with a summary of the current "settings" of the board. At this time you can do things like set the security level needed to access the board and assign an auxiliary board Sysop. To edit a parameter, just select the corresponding number and you will be able to edit the displayed value. The fields you can edit are:

1. **NAME** – The name of the board. It may be edited at any time.

2. **FILE** – The name of the bulletin file that will be used to store all bulletins for this board. It must always contain a drive specifier. Generally, the form of the filename is "Bx" where 'x' is the number of the board. Make sure you never have two boards with the some filename as they will both access the same bulletins.

3. **ACCESS** – The security flag that the user must have set so that they can access the board. If set to zero, any user can access the board. This does not affect whether they can post bulletins on the board or not.

4. **WRITE** – The security flag that the user must have set so that they can post bulletins on the board. This does not affect whether the user can access the board or not. If set to zero, this will allow any user to post on this board.

5. **AUX NUM** – The user-number of a user that will act as a Sysop for this board. This will give them power to delete anyone's messages. This allows the person to easily manage the board.

6. **AUX NAME** – Give the auxiliary Sysop a certain "title" that all of their bulletins will be posted under. This is useful in games for the administrators and for other purposes. If this field is not defined, the auxiliary Sysop's bulletins will be posted under their own name.

7. **MAX** – Sets the maximum number of bulletins that can be saved on this board. Once this limit is reached, no more bulletins can be saved unless auto-kill is enabled.

8. **AUTO KILL** – The auto-kill limit is similar to the maximum bulletins allowed on a board. When this limit is reached, and a user tries to post a new bulletin, an old bulletin will be deleted to make room for it. This is a nice way to have a board that is self-maintaining.

9. **THRESHOLD** – This is the bulletin number that will be killed when the auto-kill limit is reached. Many times you will accumulate a few bulletins that you wish to save on the board. If you wish to save bulletins 1 - 5, set the threshold to 6. This will protect the first five bulletins from being killed by the system.

Once you are done with your modifications to the board, choose Option 10 to save your changes or Option 11 to abort them. In any case, the new board will be saved. If you abort, it will be saved with the default information used. To remove a board, use the delete option. The other options are self-explanatory.

Print a List of Users

Also included within the configuration program is a utility to print a sorted list of your system users. The list can be sorted on different fields and can be limited to certain users based on security flags. You can also hide the passwords in the list, so that if you wish to give the list to someone else, you won't give away the passwords. To use the user list utility you must have a printer card installed in Slot 1.

To use the utility, select Option 8 "Sort and Print Userlist" from the main configuration menu. You will then be presented with a second menu with seven choices:

```
                - Sort and Print Userlist -


1 - Sort by user name
2 - Sort by the user number
3 - Sort by user password
4 - Sort by phone number
5 - Sort by last date on
6 - Sort by security level
7 - Return to main menu

Which? [1-7] _
```

Choose and enter the sort type you would like. You can then enter a security flag number if you would like only a partial list of users. Printing only users with Flag 2 would list all of your privileged users. Press RETURN to list all the users. If you answer "Yes" to "Hide Passwords" then asterisks (*) will be printed in the password field.

Purging Old Users

Many people call a bulletin board once or twice and never call back again. As a result, you can have a lot of old users accumulating and taking up disk space. In order to take care of this problem, the configuration program is equipped with a utility for deleting users who have not been calling the system.

The utility allows you to enter a "threshold date" which is compared to the "last date called" field of the user. If the user has not called since the threshold date, then the user will be deleted. Though you might want your local users to call at least once a month, that time frame might be unrealistic for your long distance users. By placing "&" in the phone number of these long distance users, they can have a separate threshold date. Setting a user's phone number to "000-000&0000" will place them into a second threshold category which can be set independent from the normal threshold.

Select Option 9 "Purge Users From System" from the main configuration menu. Next, enter the date threshold for normal users:

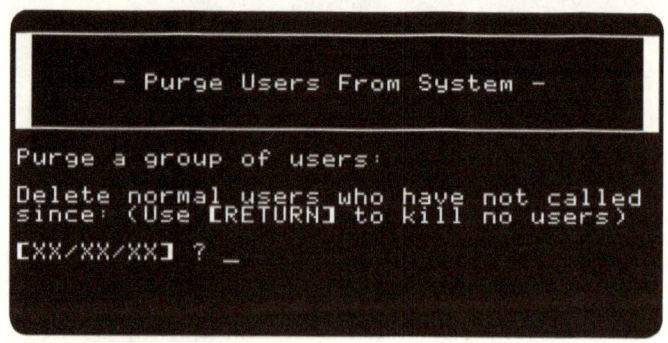

Make sure that this threshold is correct. If you enter a date in the future, the utility will delete all of your users. If you do not want to delete any normal users, just press RETURN. Second, enter the date threshold for special users (those users with a "&" in their phone number), or press RETURN if you do not want to delete any special users. Double-check your entries are correct. If everything is correct, enter "Y" and place your system disk into your second drive (if you have a floppy-based system) and press RETURN to begin the purge.

Using ACOS Utilities

There a few utilities included with the system that are written in ACOS. While running these utilities is similar to running the bulletin board, it is not exactly the same.

The two currently included utilities are "Bulletin Copy" and "New Message Fix". Both of these utilities are self-explanatory. Because of their popularity, these utilities are included in this manual, however, actual operation of these utilities is not described.

The functions of the two utilities is simple. The Bulletin Copy utility (called "BC.S" on the GBBS.SYSTEM disk) will allow a Sysop to copy bulletins from one board to another, write them into a text file on disk, delete bulletins, and some other manipulations. The New Message utility (called "NEW.MSG.FIX.S" on the GBBS.SYSTEM disk) will allow the Sysop to clean up their new message retrieval system.

Sometimes, due to a system crash or some kind of error, the New Message system will stop working correctly. It may always (or never) indicate that there are new bulletins. By running the New Message fix, the counters, pointers, etc. will all be set back to their proper settings.

To run either of these utilities, copy the utility (using the filename above) onto your boot disk (if you are using a floppy system) or onto your boot volume (if you are using mass storage).

Start to boot your system as normal, using the instructions in Chapter 2, until you come to the point in the "ACOS LOADER" where the message "STARTING MODULE (LOGON.SEG):" is displayed.

At this point, enter either "BC" or "NEW.MSG.FIX". The ".S" suffix is always left off. Then complete the normal boot procedure. Instead of the bulletin board running as normal, the utility program will be run instead.

Once execution of the program is complete, you will get the "**** RESTART S,M,Q" prompt. Press "Q" to quit to the ProDOS quit code. From this point you can run the bulletin board again and see the effect of your changes.

CHAPTER 5
ACOS Reference

General Information

Welcome to the world of ACOS. The following document was written to introduce you to ACOS and to help you learn to write your own programs or modify others written in ACOS.

ACOS is a full-featured language just like BASIC, PASCAL, FORTRAN, or any other language. It resembles BASIC more than any other language due to the fact that almost everyone involved with computers is familiar with BASIC. Since the goal was to make ACOS as easy to use as possible, it was modeled after BASIC.

This package contains a proprietary ACOS compiler which you will be using, unlike many interpreted BASICs which have their editor built-in. ACOS requires the use of some form of text editor for you to manipulate your source files. All ACOS source files are stored as text, so any editor that can modify standard text files can be used.

Writing a Program

The first thing you need to do is start the text editor or word processor you plan on using to write your code. Once you are ready, enter the following program:

```
LOOP
   PRINT "This is an ACOS program"
   PRINT "I hope it works!"
   GOTO LOOP
```

The important points to note are these: ACOS is not based around line numbers as is the BASIC language. It is free-form like PASCAL or Assembly Language. It uses labels as markers for groups of code instead of line numbers that marks the beginning of a line of code when the requirement arises to identity specific points within the program. Since your labels can have descriptive names to begin a section of code, it makes it easier to see what this code does.

Also, you can add extra blank lines at the top and bottom of a group of code to identify it more clearly. If you add comments within your code, it helps to remember what you were trying to do in that section.

There are a few rules that must be followed in order for ACOS to process your code. LABELS must *always* begin at column 0 at the left side of the screen. The rest of the code always begins in column 1. The only exception to this is the use of quotes (') to identify text. When you open a quote at the start of a print statement, all the following text will be printed to the screen until another quote is encountered. This includes normal text, any control characters and blank lines.

Once you have typed in this test program, save it to your ACOS compiler (boot volume) disk under the name "TEST.S". You must ALWAYS add a ".S" to the end of any source file for ACOS so that ACOS knows it is a "source" file. Then exit from your editor back to into BASIC.SYSTEM. Insert the disk with the ACOS compiler and prefix to that disk. Execute the ACOS compiler with the appropriate command (-ACOS, BRUN ACOS).

At this time, the ACOS loader will execute and check through the directory for any ACOS source files and do some file maintenance at the same time. You will then be asked for the name of the ACOS program to be executed. Pressing RETURN will execute the default starting program which is indicated in brackets. This default filename will differ from application to application. Type in "TEST" and RETURN. You will then see "TEST" displayed as the default filename. Enter RETURN and the compiler will start to execute.

The screen will clear and you will see a "One moment, compiling message." prompt. This means that the compiler is in the first pass of its two pass compile. After a short wait, two periods will be added. This indicates that the compiler is in its second pass. This generally

is very fast. Once the second phase is complete and has created a
new file (which in this case is called "TEST.G"), The message will
be cleared and the program will be executed. The following will be
displayed:

```
This is an ACOS program
I hope it works!
This is an ACOS program
I hope it works!
This is an ACOS program
I hope it works!

etc ...
```

The two lines will be repeated over and over until you stop the
program via the RESET key. Let's see how this program works.

The first thing that happens is that the ACOS interpreter looks at
the first line of code for a label that begins at the very leftmost column
of the screen. This tells ACOS that the first line is actually a LABEL.
A LABEL is a reference point in a program to a section of code. A
LABEL has no effect when the program flow passes through it, but it
directs the operation from the line executing from one section of code
to the beginning of the section where the LABEL is.

Execution then passes to the next line since the first has no actual
effect. ACOS looks and sees that the second line does NOT start at
the leftmost column but starts at column 1. This tells ACOS that the
data on the line is the actual program code. ACOS then looks at the
first word (which in this case was PRINT). ACOS then goes into its
internal PRINT routine as you asked.

Once within the PRINT routine, special rules take over that
govern the PRINT statement. Summing up, PRINT will display to
the console whatever text or data is between the " " marks. In this
case, it printed "This is an ACOS Program". This data was placed
within quotes to show that it was text. Once the end of the line was
encountered, execution passed to the next line.

The next line was another PRINT statement which was displayed:
"I Hope it Works!". This is the same text that you typed in when you

wrote the short program. It works in the same way as the first PRINT statement. This is the simplest form of the PRINT statement. Its function is by no means limited to this basic form since there are many other variations that can be used.

The last line of the program contained another statement to be executed by virtue that it was indented one space. This time, the STATEMENT or COMMAND was GOTO. This statement does what is called FLOW CONTROL. This is the process by which the point of execution of the program is changed from the last line executed to a new line.

When the GOTO routine is executed, it searches for the name of the LABEL and when it finds the LABEL it executes the next line of code. In this case, the label was LOOP. ACOS then looks through the program to find a label called LOOP. As it happens, that label is on the first line of the program, though it could have been in any line. The program execution point is then moved to the label LOOP, which happens to be at the beginning of the program.

Thus, the text is printed again and again. This situation is called an INFINITE LOOP. That is, the loop will never stop (unless you stop it via RESET or some such means).

After you press RESET, you will be faced with a group of choices labeled "***RESTART: S,M,Q ?". By pressing "S" you will restart the original startup program you told ACOS to execute. By pressing "M" you will restart the program in memory. In this case, they are the same, but programs can link to other programs so that the original one is different from the program now in memory.

This is helpful for debugging so you can re-start that program in memory without starting with the original program first. By pressing "Q", you will quit ACOS and return to ProDOS via the quit code.

At this point you have successfully written, compiled, and executed an ACOS program. Though this was a simple example, the steps are the some for advanced programs. The following is a summary of the steps involved in writing an ACOS program:

1. Enter some form of word or text processor that can accommodate standard text files.

2. Type in your ACOS program. All labels start at column 0 while all actual code starts at column 1.

3. Save the program to disk adding a ".S" suffix onto your filename (TEST.S) so that ACOS can identify it as an ACOS source file.

4. Execute ACOS from ProDOS via whatever commands are needed. (-ACOS, BRUN ACOS, ACOS)

5. Enter the name of the module you wish to execute if it is different from the default name. Do not add the ".S" suffix or the file will not be found.

6. The compiler will then compile and execute your program. If you execute the program again without changing the source code, the compiler will NOT recompile, it will just run the old complied code.

The following section contains information on all the data formats, variable types and disk access methods that can be used with ACOS. A working knowledge of BASIC is recommended to help you along. If you don't know any other language, try and use the examples as much as possible. They will be the best teacher. Also try modifying existing code. This is another easy way to learn.

Program Structure

Under ACOS, the structure of a program is very "freeform". That is, the compiler is very tolerant of different styles of programming. You are allowed to add blank lines and comments anywhere in your code for ease of reading. Any line within an ACOS source program must be in one of the following formats:

Blank line   If the line is blank, this line will be skipped by the compiler. Blank lines are a good way to separate blocks of your code apart from other blocks for ease of reading.

Comment Line   By placing a semi-colon (;) as the first character of the line in column 0, all data until the end of the line will be ignored. In this way, you can enter comments so that when you come back to work on a program, you will have some idea of what you were trying to accomplish.

Label Line   By entering just a keyword of your choice starting at column 0 of the line, you can enter a label. The first character of a label must be alphabetic. The rest can contain alphanumeric characters. Any characters except ":" and unprintable characters are okay. The first eight characters of the label are significant. That is, the labels TEST and TEST2 are considered different labels by ACOS while SHOWFILE2 and SHOWFILE8 would appear the same to ACOS since the first eight characters are the same.

Statement Line A statement line is always indented 1 space from the left side. That is, it starts at column 1, not column 0 like the previous line types. Statements are just entered on the line in the order you want them executed. If you want multiple statements on a line, separate the statements with a colon (:). Statements may be typed in either upper, lower or mixed case.

Special Characters

There are several special characters that ACOS recognizes within your program code and uses them for different purposes. The following list shows characters that have special meanings to ACOS. Any character, including those below, can be displayed by the program without problem, they just have special meanings when encountered outside the PRINT statement.

Character   Meaning

	Space or blank
=	Equal Sign used for assignment statements
+	Plus Sign used for adding strings and variables
-	Minus Sign used for subtraction
*	Asterisk Multiply Sign used for multiplication
/	Slash used for division
(	Open Parenthesis used to begin a function
)	Close Parenthesis used to end a function
$	Dollar Sign used to indicate a string function
,	Comma used as a data separator
;	Semicolon used for text formatting and comments
:	Colon used as a statement separator
"	Double Quote for string delimiter
'	Apostrophe delimiter for block text formatting
\	Backslash or newline character
<	Less Than used with IF
>	Greater Than used with IF

Reserved Words

Under ACOS, certain reserved words have predefined meanings. These words all correspond to ACOS statements, functions and operands. When encountered, they will be executed as an ACOS command. They may NOT be used for variable names.

It is always best if you separate reserved words from data, or each other, by the use of a space or a colon or whatever special characters the particular command syntax allows.

A key factor in writing a good program is making sure you can understand what you wrote. For example,"PRINT A$;B$,C PEEK(27):HOME" uses a (;), a (.), a ( ) space, and a (:) between data.

The following is a list of reserved words:

ABS	HOME	PUBLIC
ADDINT	IF	PUSH
AND	INFO	RAM
APPEND	INPUT	RAM2
ASC	INSTR	RANDOM
BYTE	KEY	READ
CALL	KILL	READY
CHR$	LEFT$	RECALL
CLEAR	LEN	RESUME
CLOCK	LINK	RETURN
CLOSE	LOG	REWIND
COPY	MARK	RIGHT$
CREATE	MID$	RND$

CRUNCH	MOD	SET
DATE$	MODEM	SETINT
ECHO	MOVE	SIZE
EDIT	MSG	STEP
ELSE	NEXT	STORE
END	NIBBLE	STR$
EOF	NOT	TEXT
EOR	ON ERROR	THEN
ERR	ON NOCAR	TIME$
FILL	OPEN	TO
FLAG	OR	TONE
FMTDATE$	PDL	UPDATE
FOR	PEEK	USE
FREE	POKE	VAL
GET	POP	WHEN$
GOSUB	POSITION	WIDTH
GOTO	PRINT	WRITE

Variables

One of the most powerful parts of any language is the use of VARIABLES. ACOS contains two basic variable types. The common ways of using them are listed below:

Numeric   Under ACOS, numeric variables are just integers. Floating point numbers are not supported. ACOS is not a good language if your application demands heavy math support. The integers are in the range -32767 to +32768. Numbers outside this range will either "wrap-around" or give on OVERFLOW ERROR. Numeric variables are represented as names of your choice. They must start with an alphabetical character, but can contain any alphanumeric characters that you desire. For instance, ABC, Z7, AS76D are all legal numeric variables.

String   Under ACOS, string variables are the same as they are under most BASICs. They can be between 0 and 255 characters in length. They can accept any type of characters (control, upper case, lower case, numeric, etc.), and can be manipulated in a number of ways. String variables must start with an alphabetical character and can contain any alphanumeric character as can a numeric variable. However, the variable name must be terminated by a dollar sign. For example, ZQ$, A7$, NAME$ are all legal string variables.

Unlike many BASICs, ACOS does NOT support arrays. Due to speed and memory considerations, array support is impractical. Fortunately, ACOS has been engineered to handle large groups of data that will out-perform most normal array systems.

Under ACOS, variable names can be of any length, though only the first two characters are used within ACOS for identification. For example, you can use the variable VOTE throughout your program without a problem. Internally though, ACOS only looks at it as VO.

As a result, if you have a second variable named VOLUME, internally, it will be the same as VOTE.

Thus, the two variables will be the same as far as ACOS is concerned. The ability to use variable names greater than two characters is only for your reading convenience.

You can assign a variable a value the same way you do in any BASIC. You can use: LET VOTE=1 to set the variable VO to a value of 1. As a shortcut, you can just say VO=1, and ACOS will figure out what you mean. The LET is on optional operator.

When assigning a string variable to an absolute value, the string to be assigned must be enclosed in quotes and must be no more than 255 characters in length. NAME$ = "STEVE WOZNIAK" is a legal string assignment.

Arithmetic Operators

There are several standard arithmetic operators that can be applied to numeric and string variables. Though they are somewhat limited in nature under ACOS, most common functions can be accommodated.

Addition   A=B+C or A=B+5 or A=3+7 are all legal operators. Whenever a number is needed for whatever purpose, an equation may be substituted within its place. A$=B$+C$ or A$=B$+"HMMM" or A$="This Is"+"A Test" are all legal string addition commands. Under string addition, the contents of the second string are appended onto the contents of the first.

Subtraction   A=B-C or A=B-5 or A=3-7 are all legal operators. It is very similar to using the addition operator. There is no string subtraction operator.

Multiplication A=B*C or A=B*5 or A=3*7 are all legal operators. If you combine multiplication / division operands with addition / subtraction operands, the multiplication / division will be executed first. For example: 4+5*3 = 19 (not 27).

Division   A=B/C or A=B/5 or A=3/7 are all legal operators. Since ACOS is an Integer-based language, when using division operands, the results are rounded to the nearest integer and remainders are thrown away. Thus: 10/2=5. 10/3=3. 10/7=1. 10/11=0.

Modulo   A=B MOD C or A=B MOD 5 or A=3 MOD 7 are all legal operators. The MOD operand is a sub-function of division. Instead of returning the quotient (as with division), the remainder is returned. Thus: 10 MOD 2=0. 10 MOD 3=1. 10 MOD 7=3.

Grouping   Mathematical functions in ACOS are generally
evaluated left to right. When performing complex
mathematical operations, parenthesis are required
for operand order control. Arguments within a set of
parenthesis are always executed first. You may also
nest several levels of parentheses if necessary. (See
"Logical Operators" on page 71 for further details).
Thus: ((3+4)*5)/(3+4) is evaluated in the following
steps:

Step 1. (7*5) / (3+4)
Step 2. 35 / (3+4)
Step 3. 35 / 7
Step 4. The result is 5.

Relational Operators

Relational operators are used to compare two values and return a true / false result. Strings may be compared with other strings, but not to numbers. The same is true for numbers. A "TRUE" result is returned as the value 1 while a "FALSE" result is returned as the value 0. The following are the legal relational operators:

Operator	Relation	Example
=	Equality	X=Y
<> or ><	Inequality	X<>Y or X><Y
<	Less Than	X<Y
>	Greater Than	X>Y
<= or =<	Less Than or Equal To	X<=Y or X=<Y
>= or =>	Greater Than or Equal To	X>=Y or X=>Y

Examples: (1=0) with the result of false or (0), (1=1) with the result of true or (1), (5<4) with the result of false or (0), (5>4) with the result of true or (1), (7<7) with the result of false or (0), (7>=7) with the result of true or (1).

You may always substitute more complex variables in place of simple variables. You can replace ((X) > (Y)) with a more complex expression like ((4+5*6)>(3/4+12)) or expressions that are even more complex. If you do have a complex expression on a side, you should put parentheses around it to separate it from the relational operator so it is processed as one side.

When used in conjunction with the IF statement, you have one of the most powerful statements within ACOS. When used with the IF statement, you have a conditional branch, the single most important program execution statement.

Logical Operators

Logical operators perform simple logic operations on numeric values. They can be used to increase the power of the IF statement by allowing more conditions to be evaluated. Under their simplest form, logical operators work with true (1) and false (0) values. The following truth tables show the results of all the possible logical operators in action.

Z = NOT X			Z = X AND Y			Z = X OR Y	
X	Z	X	Y	Z	X	Y	Z
1	0	1	1	1	1	1	1
0	1	1	0	0	1	0	1
0	1	0	1	0	0	1	1
		0	0	0	0	0	0

The following examples show the IF statement being used with the relational and logical operators:

```
IF (X=5) AND (Y=9) GOTO label

IF (NAME$="SAM") AND (UN=1) GOTO label

IF NOT ((A=3) OR (8=4)) GOTO label
```

Again, it is important to use parentheses when complex equations are being evaluated so that ACOS can understand the order the operand is processed. Since execution order is normally sequential, without grouping, ACOS will be on its own to decide what order you wanted to do things. Many times it will guess correctly, but occasionally it will guess wrong. Using grouping is on easy way to avoid this problem.

Print Statements

The two most frequently used and versatile statements are PRINT and INPUT. These are the basic means by which you input data into variables and print the data out to the screen. Due to the frequency of use, a basic understanding of these two statements is very important.

The PRINT statement has the function of taking data and displaying it on the console/modem. There are many options in PRINT that can be used.

The basic form of print is PRINT (expression). In the simplest form you can use PRINT (any absolute data). This would include numbers (PRINT 563) or text within quotes (PRINT "HELLO"). To include multiple arguments, you need not even separate them, though a space or semi-colon between them makes it easier to read: PRINT "THE VALUE 4+5=";9.

Of course, in place of absolute data, you can have statements, equations, and variables. For example, the above print statement could be redone as: PRINT "THE VALUE 4+5=";4+5. If you wish to print a function, enclose the function within the print statement . For example, PRINT PEEK(456) would display the contents of memory location 456.

To print a variable just include the name of the variable in the PRINT statement. PRINT NAME$ would print the contents of NAME$ on the screen. To combine multiple statements, just use the semicolon or a space. PRINT NAME$;UN;PEEK(456);4+5 would display all the above data.

There are several special characters that can be used with the PRINT statement to format the data. If you use a comma instead of a semicolon, the comma will be displayed. There is also a print-at character (@) that can be used. PRINT @5,0;"HELLO" will display the word HELLO at horizontal location line 5, vertical location column 0.

Input Statements

The INPUT statement is used to enter data in variables from the console/modem by the user. It also has a quick directive so the text can be displayed (like a PRINT statement) before the data is entered.

In its simplest form, INPUT is used to enter either a string or numeric variable from the console/modem. INPUT NAME$ would wait for the user to enter a string from the keyboard. That string would then be put into NAME$.

To enter multiple variables, separate the variable names with either the comma or the back-slash character. When you separate variables with a comma, the input must correspond to the number of commas used in the input. For example, INPUT A,B,C would wait for three numbers to be entered. Typing 1,2,3 would enter 1 for A, 2 for B, and 3 for C.

If you enter a backslash between variables, then each value must be on a separate line. This avoids having to do multiple INPUT statements all in a row. Thus, INPUT AS\BS, would enter two lines worth of data into the two strings.

To display a prompt (like a PRINT statement) in advance of the input, you can put any text within quotes. For example: INPUT "NAME ->";NAME$ would display the prompt NAME -> and would then wait for your input. Of course, you can also use multiple variables with the prompt as above.

Disk Access

Under ACOS, accessing disk drives is similar to that of CP/M. It does not change from implementation to implementation, even when moved to another computer and/or operating system, or even when using the same computer with a different operating system.

Under ACOS, there are a maximum of 12 different drives labeled "A:" though "L:". Under ProDOS "A:" drive might be "/PROFILE/ SYSTEM".

For any drive, there are up to 99 subsets to that drive. For example, "A3:" can be a legal drive. If you had "A:" defined as "/PROFILE/SYSTEM" then "A3:" would try to find the directory "/PROFILE/SYSTEM3". The base drives are defined within the ACOS config program.

To change drives within ACOS, you can always prefix the filename with the drive specifier. Whenever you access a drive, the default drive is set to the last drive used. Also, to set the default drive without doing any real disk access, the LOG statement can be used. For example, the syntax for LOG is LOG "drive spec" or LOG "B".

Disk Files

The last part of this introduction deals with using disk files. This is one of the most important and powerful features of ACOS. You can OPEN a file, manipulate the data within, and then CLOSE the file. If you wish to use a new file, the CREATE statement can be used. If you wish to delete an old file, the KILL statement can be used. The disk commands are:

APPEND	MARK
CLOSE	OPEN
CREATE	POSITION
INPUT	PRINT
KILL	READ
LOG	WRITE

The first thing to do is open the file. You use the "OPEN #channel,filename" statement. There are two disk channels that may be used. The two channels are 1 and 2. Only one file per disk channel may be open at a time. Thus, there is a maximum of two files open at any one time. The filename format differs from operating system to operating system. For example: OPEN #1,"USERS" would open the file USERS on disk channel 1.

Once you have opened a disk file, all further access is done with reference to the disk channel of the file you opened. At this point, the following commands can be used to access the file:

APPEND #channel – Sets the file so that all new data written to the file will be appended onto the end of the file.

INPUT #channel, expression – Like the normal INPUT statement except that input will be taken from the open disk file instead of the console/modem.

MARK (channel) = current byte location within file – With the MARK statement, you can select the actual byte number from the beginning of the file. This is generally not used.

current location within file = MARK (channel) – In this form, the MARK function will return the current pointer location within a disk file.

POSITION #channel, record size, record number, offset – The POSITION statement is used in conjunction with random access files. If you wanted to use a file as random access with records of 128 bytes, you can use: POSITION #1,128,record number. The offset argument is optional and defaults to zero if not used.

PRINT #channel, expression – The PRINT statement can be used in the normal way except that the output will be directed to the disk file instead of the console/modem .

READ #channel, memory location, number of bytes to read – This is a direct disk to memory transfer method. A maximum of 255 bytes can be read at a time.

WRITE #channel, memory location, number of bytes to write – This is a direct memory to disk transfer method. A maximum of 255 bytes can be written at a time.

After you are finished with the file you are using, you must issue a CLOSE command to tell ACOS you are finished with the file. If you add a device number (#1) after the CLOSE statement, only that channel will be closed. If you just issue a CLOSE without an argument, all open files will be closed. If you are only using one file at a time, it is generally a good practice to issue just a CLOSE command with no channel number.

ACOS Compiler Specs

Hardware Required:	Apple II series
Memory Required:	64K
Operating System:	ProDOS
Hardware Supported:	Printer, Modem, Display Cards, Clock
Total Program Space:	19.5K
Total Variable Space:	19.5K – program space
Internal Editor Space:	4K
Disk Channels:	2 (+1 for message base use)
RAM Drive:	64 bytes
RAM2 Drive:	64 bytes
Scratch RAM:	192 bytes
Compiler Info:	Standard 2 pass compiler built on assembler principles for label-oriented languages

Pass 1 Info:

Compiler pass 1 takes text source code and tokenizes all statements and functions into single byte tokens. All text and symbols are marked as such for fast recognition. All label addresses are stored into a table. All label references are put into a separate table. Tokenized code is generated into memory without addresses.

Pass 2 Info:

Compiler pass 2 goes through the label reference table and searches for the address of the desired routine. If a match is not found, a LABEL NOT FOUND message is displayed. Otherwise, the address is saved into the second table. Afterwards, all references that were found are inserted into the actual code. The compiled code is then saved to disk.

Code Execution:

Actual code execution is based on a "fetch-and-go" method. Each token is fetched from compiled code. The routine is then found via a lookup table and is executed. When label references are made, the address is already known so no time is taken searching for the given label.

Command List

1.1   ADDINT

Syntax: ADDINT (string 1 [,string 1...])

Example: ADDINT ("A", "B", "C")

The ADDINT command will add more keys to the existing
interrupt keys table. Previous keys will not be cleared. The function
of the keys is the same as with the SETINT command.

1.2   APPEND

Syntax: APPEND #device

Example: APPEND #1

The APPEND statement is generally used to add data to an
existing file. If you issue an APPEND statement, the file pointer will
be moved to the end of the file. All extra data will then be tacked
on to the end. You can also find out the length of a file by doing on
APPEND and then using the MARK function. MARK will then return
the length of the file in bytes.

1.3   ASC

Syntax: expression=ASC(string1)

Example: get a$:print "Input was: "ASC(a$)

The ASC function is used to determine the number of the code
representing the character under the ASCII definition table. An ASCII
table can be found in the Appendices section.

1.4 **BYTE**

Syntax: BYTE=expression
BYTE=number
BYTE(number)
BYTE(number)=number256

Example: p=BYTE; BYTE=ram2; BYTE(4)=12

The BYTE function is similar to the FLAG function. It is a low overhead data storage unit. Just point to where in memory you want the data to be stored using the first syntax, and you can then access the data using the second and third syntaxes. Use care when using this command – it could corrupt memory. This command has no argument overflow checking and no address checking. A bad address could trigger softswitches. argument = argument mod 256.

1.5 **CALL**

Syntax: CALL memloc

Example: call 768

The CALL statement is used to jump to a machine language routine residing in memory. The argument is the starting address of the routine in decimal format. Use care when using this command – it could have unintended results.

1.6 **CHR$**

Syntax: string=CHR$(ascii code (,# chars))

Example: md$=CHR$(36,39)

The CHRS statement is useful for generating characters that are not easily generated from the keyboard such as control characters. The ASCII code is a number in the range 0-127 that represents the desired character in the ASCII character chart. If you wish to generate a group of the same character, add a second argument with the number of characters that you wish to be generated.

1.7   **CLEAR**

Syntax: CLEAR
               CLEAR #device

Example: CLEAR; CLEAR #9

The forms of clear share only one thing in common – they both clear data in one form or another. In the first syntax, without an argument, CLEAR will reset all the variables to nil, and clear both the FOR-NEXT and GOSUB-RETURN stacks. It is a good idea to issue a clear statement at the beginning of your program. In its second syntax, CLEAR is used to clear out device buffers. The legal device channels are 8,9,10.

1.8   **CLOCK**

Syntax: CLOCK(0)
               expression=CLOCK(1)
               CLOCK(2)=expression

Example: a=CLOCK(1); CLOCK(2)=nibble(1)*600

The CLOCK function/statement is used for setting a time limit. It can also be used to find out how long someone has been using the system. If the argument is out of range, this function does nothing. Can result in a problem when writing. The following options are available:

CLOCK(0)   Used to reset the clock time to zero. It should be executed when your program begins.

CLOCK(1)   Returns the number of seconds that a user has been connected. Divide this number by 60 to find how many minutes they have been connected.

CLOCK(2)   You need to set CLOCK(2) equal to the number of minutes you want as a time limit, or 0 for no limit.

1.9   **CLOSE**

Syntax: CLOSE
               CLOSE #device

Example: CLOSE; CLOSE #1

The CLOSE command is used to close a disk file after you are
done with it. If you give a device channel with the close command,
only that file will be closed. If you use CLOSE by itself, all open
files will be closed. If the device number is specified, then the device
specifier "#" is required.

1.10   **COPY**

Syntax: COPY [(lines)] filename [,#device]
               COPY [(lines)] #device [,#device]

Example: COPY "b:help.system";COPY(50) #1,#7

The COPY command is used for displaying and copying
information from device to device. The first argument is optional. It
is the number of lines of text to be copied. If you wish to show only a
certain number of lines, you can include the number to be shown. The
second argument can be a filename, in which case, the file is opened
and input is taken from that file, or it can be a device. The second
device is optional. If present, all output will be routed there, otherwise
it will be displayed to the modem/console. The second argument may
not be another filename. If you wish to copy to a file, open the file
with the OPEN command and copy to that device.

1.11   **CREATE**

Syntax: CREATE filename

Example: CREATE "a:testfile"

The CREATE statement is used to create an empty file on disk.
The new file can then be opened, read, and written to, just as any
other file would be. This is the only way to create a file under ACOS.
Unlike some other BASICs, ACOS will NOT create a file using the
OPEN command.

1.12   **CRUNCH**

Syntax: CRUNCH

Example: CRUNCH

The CRUNCH statement is used in conjunction with the MSG
commands. It is used to "CRUNCH" together a message file in which
messages have been killed. This allows you to maintain a sequential
message file and get rid of all blank deleted entries that might be there.

1.13   **DATE$**

Syntax: string=DATE$
               DATE$=string

Example: I$=DATE$; DATE$="04/19/87"

The DATE$ function returns the current date in MM/DD/YY
format. The input will be taken from whatever device is configured
as a clock. If 00/00/00 is returned, then there is no clock in the
system and the date has not been set. If DATE$ is set to a string in
the MM/DD/YY format, and there is no clock in the system then that
string will be used for the date since no other is known.

1.14   **ECHO**

Syntax: ECHO=string1
               ECHO=""

Example: ECHO="X"; ECHO=""

The ECHO statement is used to set the echo character to be used
with the INPUT statement. Once the echo has been set, that character
will be sent each time a user types a character when entering text.
The ECHO statement in the second syntax will reset the echo to the
character that is being typed.

1.15   **EDIT**

Syntax: EDIT(number)

Example: EDIT(3)=40; If not EDIT(2) return

The EDIT statement is the command used to interface ACOS with
its editor. With the different EDIT statements you can clear the editor,
see how much space is free, etc. All the legal calls to the editor are:

> **Edit(0)** – Clear the editor. There will be a total of 4096 bytes
> free after a clear takes place.

> **Edit(1)** – Enter the editor. If no data is present, the editor will
> start to accept input right away. If other data is present, the editor
> will start in its prompt mode.

> **Edit(2)** – This is a function that returns the number of bytes
> used within the editor. If this number is zero, the editor is empty.

> **Edit(3)** – This is used to set the video width to be used within
> the editor. Any value from 1 to 255 is legal. The most often used
> widths are 32, 40, 64, 80 and 128. All operations within the editor
> will be based around this width. You can also read the current
> width using it as a function.

Edit(4) – This used to set the Backspace Mode that the editor will use. Certain modes allow more control than others. Mode 0 indicates that the actual mode is not known. The editor will work fine, but some functions will be disabled. Under Mode 1, the editor assumes that the user has a non-destructible backspace. This allows all the editor functions to be used and is how the local console is setup. Mode 2 tells the editor that the user has a 'destructible' backspace. Under this mode, some functions are disabled but the editor speeds up other functions. This function is read/write

Edit(5) – Returns the starting address of the editor in memory.

1.16   **END**

Syntax: END

Example: END

The END statement is used to cleanly terminate execution of a program. END statements can be used anywhere in your code and when encountered will return ACOS to its restart state.

1.17   **EOF**

Syntax: nexprs=EOF(dev)

Example: if eof(1) close #1:return

The EOF function is a Boolean operator that becomes true when the end of the file has been reached. It is most often used in conjunction with on IF-THEN statement. It can be used with either device channels #1 or #2.

1.18   **ERR**

Syntax: nexprs=ERR

Example: if err=11 print "Can't divide by 0"

ERR returns the number of the error that last occurred. See the "Error Messages" section for a list of errors and their numbers.

1.19   **FILL**

Syntax: FILL start,length,data

Example: FILL ram,34,0

The FILL statement is used to fill an area of memory with some byte of data. Generally it is used to zero out memory. START is a 16 bit memory address, LENGTH is an 8-bit (0-255) number, and DATA is the byte that will be used to fill memory.

1.20   **FLAG**

Syntax: expression=FLAG
                 FLAG=number
                 FLAG(number)
                 FLAG(number)=number1

Example: FLAG=ram2; FLAG(3)=1; z=FLAG(7)

The FLAG function is a low overhead way to store 1-bit information. You just need to point the FLAG function to a point in memory that you wish to store your data in, and you can manipulate as many flags as you need. Each byte of memory can contain eight flags. To setup the FLAG function, use the first syntax to point the function to a point in memory where the flags will be stored. Once the pointer is setup, you can use FLAG just like a variable using the second and third syntax for reading and writing the flags. Use care when using this command – it could corrupt memory. This command has no argument overflow checking and no address checking. A bad address could trigger softswitches. argument = argument mod 256.

1.21   **FMTDATE$**

Syntax: string=FMTDATE$

Example: i$=FMTDATE$

The FMTDATE$ function returns the current date in "Mon, DD, YYYY" format. The input will be taken from whatever device is configured as a clock. If there is no clock in the system, use the DATE$ function to set the current date.

1.22   **FOR**

Syntax: FOR numvar=number TO number STEP
               number;NEXT

Example: FOR X = 1 TO 11 STEP 2: ...... :NEXT

The FOR statement is one of the most powerful parts of the ACOS language. It allows one to do a loop a specified number of times without using labels and counters. Using a FOR loop is easy. Just place the line at the beginning of the code you want to loop through and select a variable for a counter <numvar> and insert into the line. The number TO number is the range of the loop. The first number contains the value of the counter the first time through the loop. The second number is the value that the counter must reach before the loop terminates. The STEP argument is optional. When left off, the loop will execute in increments of 1. The STEP statement can be used to set a different increment.

1.23   **FREE**

Syntax: FREE

Example: FREE

The FREE statement is used to force the system 'garbage collection' routine to take effect. It clears all old strings out of memory and packs things together. Normally, this is done automatically by the system whenever it is needed and whenever a LINK statement is executed.

1.24   **GET**

Syntax: GET varstr

Example: GET a$

The GET statement is used to get a single key press from the keyboard. When encountered, the system will wait until a key is pressed. The key will be returned in <varstr>. Control characters will not be filtered as they are with INPUT.

1.25   **GOSUB**

Syntax: GOSUB label

Example: GOSUB mail

The GOSUB statement is similar to the GOTO statement in that it is used to change the execution point within the program. However, before ACOS looks for the label, it saves the current execution address so that it may be returned to. The new address is then fetched and execution goes on from that point until a RETURN statement is encountered. At that time, execution will go back to the point right after the GOSUB statement. As its function indicates, GOSUB is an abbreviation of GO SUBroutine.

1.26   **GOTO**

Syntax: GOTO label

Example: GOTO system

The GOTO statement is used to change the execution point within a program. When a GOTO is encountered, ACOS will find the point in the program with the appropriate label and start execution at that new point. It the label is not within the loaded program module, you will get a LABEL NOT FOUND error.

1.27   **HOME**

Syntax: HOME

Example: HOME

The home statement will clear the local screen and place the cursor in the upper left hand corner of the screen. HOME will NOT clear data outside the text window. To clear the entire screen, issue a TEXT statement previous to the HOME statement.

1.28   **IF**

Syntax: IF argument [THEN] statement:[ELSE] statement

Example: IF info(6) THEN a=0 ELSE a=1

The IF statement is one of the most powerful statements in the entire ACOS language. It gives the system the power of decision. With it, you can evaluate an argument and take appropriate action. The argument can either be simple or complex. The THEN statement is generally optional unless you are doing a variable declaration of some kind following the argument. If you are, then the system can think that the declaration is part of the argument unless a THEN is

included. Unlike some BASICs, where a line number can follow a
THEN, under ACOS you may NOT follow a THEN with a label. You
must use 'IF arg THEN GOTO label' or 'IF arg GOTO label' instead.

In addition, the ACOS language also supports the ELSE directive.
With the ELSE statement, you can set up such that IF the argument is
true, THEN do a statement or group of statements separated by colons.
ELSE if the argument was false, do the following set of statements.
If the argument was true and the first set of statements was executed,
when the ELSE statement is reached, control will pass to the next line.

1.29   **INFO**

Syntax: expression=INFO(option)
               INFO(option)=expression

Example: sp=INFO(1); INFO(4)=1

INFO can be used as either a statement or as a function. It
is really a catch-all in nature. Many values that are more or less
unrelated are returned. Writing to read-only items is not checked, and
could cause problems. The following table gives the meaning of all
the INFO data:

Argument	R/W	Function
INFO(0)	R	Is there a caller online? (0=No)
INFO(1)	R	Capacity of current msg file.
INFO(2)	R	Callers baud rate / 300 (1=300)
INFO(3)	R / W	Current number of nulls.
INFO(4)	W	Top screen stat. (1=Chat, 2=Exec)
INFO(5)	R / W	Executive user is online. (1=Yes)
INFO(6)	R	# of blocks in bit-map.

1.30 **INPUT**

Syntax: INPUT [#device,] [@number,] [\]
["text"] variable [{,\}variable..]

Example: INPUT a,a$; INPUT #1,a$\b$; INPUT
@2,a$; INPUT \"Name: ",n$

The INPUT statement is one of the most powerful and widely
used statements in the ACOS language. It is in its simplest form, the
opposite of the PRINT statement. The INPUT statement is broken
down into four different parts. The first part is the input device to
be used. When omitted, input is taken from the console / modem,
otherwise input is taken from that device. The second part is the input
mode. There is a restrictive mode placed on the input so that the input
data is what you desire. For example, you can set upper case only
via the mode. Other mode options are listed below. The third part
of the INPUT statement is the prompt. The prompt is basically just a
text string that will be printed prior to getting the input. The new line
character "\" can be used at the beginning of the text. The last part
of the INPUT statement is the variable list. This is a list of variables
that will be assigned the input. Each variable in the list is separated
by either a comma, or a backslash. If separated by a comma, then
the actual typed input must be divided by a comma. If divided by a
backslash, then the text must be separated by a carriage return. INPUT
mode numbers that are out of range revert to 0.

Input Default	Set the input mode to uppercase. Don't accept a blank line.
Input Mode 0	Set the input mode to uppercase. Don't accept a blank line. Just return the first character.
Input Mode 1	Set the input mode to uppercase. Don't accept a blank line. Don't accept any commas within the line.
Input Mode 2	Set the input mode to uppercase. Blank lines will be accepted.
Input Mode 3	Accept everything in both upper and lowercase.
Input Mode 4	Will throw out any commas entered in the input.

1.31   **INSTR**

Syntax: expression=INSTR(string,string[,start])

Example: IF INSTR("C","ABCABC",4) print "C was found past
              position 4"

The INSTR function is used to search within a string, beginning at an optional starting position, for the existence of another string. The first string is that string which you are searching for. The second string is what will be searched. The case of the text will be ignored. The function will return the number of the first character where the match was found. If the function returns zero, no match was found. KEY argument reverts to 0 if greater than 3.

1.32   **KEY**

Syntax: expression=KEY(0)
              expression=KEY(1)
              expression=KEY(2)
              expression=KEY(3)

Example: if KEY(1) print\ "stop char pressed"

The KEY function is used to check and see what if any keys have been pressed. It is generally used to check to see if a routine needs to be interrupted and is used in conjunction with the SETINT and ADDINT statements. This routine does not wait for a key. It returns either a zero for no key or the ASCII value of the key. In the KEY(1) form, a non-zero byte will be returned if the key pressed was the 'File Stop' character defined in the config program. In the KEY(2) form, a non-zero byte will be returned if the pressed key is the 'File Next' key defined in config. In the KEY(3) form, a non-zero byte will be returned if the key pressed is in the interrupt table defined by SETINT and ADDINT.

1.33   **KILL**

Syntax: KILL filename
               KILL #MSG(expression)

Example: KILL "b:testfile"; KILL #MSG(25)

The KILL statement can be used in two different ways. In both ways, it is used to delete data. In its first form with the filename, it will delete the file from disk. In its second form, it will kill a message within the currently active message base. After using KILL on a message, it is always a good idea to follow it with an UPDATE.

1.34   **LEFT$**

Syntax: string=LEFT$(string,length)

Example: print "Month:" LEFT$(date$,2)

The LEFT$ function is used to change a string variable into a partial string. More specifically, it will return LENGTH number of characters starting at the LEFT side of the source string. This function has no argument checking. argument = argument mod 256.

1.35   **LEN**

Syntax: expression=LEN(string)

Example: print "ABC is ";LEN("ABC");" chars long"

The LEN statement is used to determine the length of a string. The returned length will be in the range from 0 to 255.

1.36 **LINK**

Syntax: LINK filename [,string-label]

Example: LINK "a:main.seg";"main"

The link statement is one of the most powerful statements in the ACOS language. This statement will allow two program segments to be linked together. It is in this way that the problem of not enough memory space is dealt with. When you design your programs, make them so that you can link the main segments together and the memory savings will be great.

The filename argument is mandatory and is in standard filename syntax. If you wish execution to begin at a point other than the beginning of the module, then add on a comma followed by the name of the label IN STRING FORM. The label must be enclosed in quotes or must be in a string. Ex: LINK "A:MSG.SEG","BULLETINS". You must also make use of the PUBLIC command within the segment you are linking to so that the label's address is available to the link command.

1.37 **LOG**

Syntax: LOG drivespec

Example: LOG "a:"

The LOG statement simply changes the default disk drive to the <drivespec> drive. If the drive is not legal, a BAD DRIVE SPECIFIER error will occur.

1.38   **MARK**

Syntax: expression=MARK(device)
               MARK(device)=number

Example: a=MARK(1); MARK(2)=0

The MARK function will allow you to either set or check the point at which a file is doing i/o. If you want to go to the beginning of a file, you would issue a MARK(1)=0 assuming it was file 1. MARK has a second function in that it can be used to see if a file exists. Normally ACOS will not generate an error if a file does not exist, so it can be hard to tell if there is one. To see if a file exists:

```
OPEN # 1,filename
IF NOT MARK(1)  PRINT "FILE  EXISTS"
CLOSE #1
```

1.39   **MID$**

Syntax: string=MIDS(string,start [,length])

Example: print "char 2 is";MID$("ABC",2,1)

The MID$ function is put part of one string into another. It can be used in two forms. In the first, giving just a source string and a starting character number, the new string will be assigned the contents of the original string starting at the start character. If the optional length argument is added, then only that number of characters will be returned. This function has no argument checking. argument = argument mod 256.

1.40   **MODEM**

Syntax: MODEM(number)

Example: MODEM(1)

   The MODEM statement has many functions including waiting
for a call, hanging up, and initializing the modem. The number in
the syntax represents the desired modem function. The following list
contains all the modem functions.

   MODEM(0) – This command will wait for an incoming call
   and establishes a connection. Execution will continue when
   either a call is connected, or the user goes into local mode.

   MODEM(1) – This command causes the modem to hang up.
   All further output will be directed to the console only.

   MODEM(2) – Not documented. Places modem into active
   state allowing for commands to be sent to it.

1.41   **MOVE**

Syntax: MOVE start,length TO destination

Example: MOVE ram,34 TO ram2

   The MOVE statement is used to move segments of memory
around. The only limitation is that only a maximum of 255 bytes
can be moved at a time. Always be careful when moving around
memory. If you move over some memory that is use by ACOS, some
unpredictable things can happen. Both START and DESTINATION
are 16 bit memory addresses while LENGTH is an 8 bit [0-255]
number.

1.42 **MSG**

Syntax: expression=MSG(number)
            MSG(number)=expression
            device={#MSG(number)}

Example: if MSG(un) print "You have mail.";
            MSG(un)=1; copy #MSG(4)

The MSG function is a specialized function for the ACOS message handling routines. Once a message file has been opened via the READY statement, the MSG function is used to access individual messages within the message file. The MSG function has two radically different syntaxes. Under the first and second syntax, it is being used to access and set information about a message. For each message, you can maintain one number that gives information about it via the MSG function. The MSG(0) function returns the number of messages within the message file and may not be changed. To access a message, it is used as a device channel. While to show the editor COPY #8 would suffice, since the message file is made up of many messages, it is necessary to tell which message you want to work with. COPY #MSG(3) would show message number three within the currently open message file.

1.43 **NEXT**

Syntax: NEXT

Example: FOR X=1 TO 10: ...... :NEXT

The NEXT statement is used to set the ending boundary of a FOR-NEXT loop. Unlike with some versions of BASIC, the NEXT statement does not need to be followed with the name of the variable that is being used in the loop. You may also have multiple NEXTs for a single FOR statement. To end a loop early, just set the variable that is used in the loop to its final value and then execute a NEXT statement. This will terminate a loop early.

1.44   **NIBBLE**

Syntax: expression=NIBBLE
               NIBBLE=number
               NIBBLE(number)
               NIBBLE(number)=number 16

Example :   p=NIBBLE; NIBBLE=ram2; NIBBLE(1)=3

The NIBBLE function is similar to the FLAG function in that it is a low overhead data storage method. With the NIBBLE function you can store 4-bit numbers that have the range 0-15. Use the first syntax of NIBBLE to point to the point in memory where the data will be stored. Use the second and third syntaxes to read and write the actual data. Use care when using this command – it could corrupt memory. This command has no argument overflow checking and no address checking. A bad address could trigger softswitches. argument = argument mod 256.

1.45   **NOT**

Syntax: expression=NOT expression

Example: If NOT edit(2) return: a=NOT b

The NOT operator is a Boolean logic operator. It changes the value of an expression from true to false or from false to true. In Boolean logic, false is considered to be zero while not false, or true, is considered to be any other number. The NOT operator is most commonly used in IF statements.

1.46   **ON ERROR**

Syntax: ON ERROR GOTO label
               ON ERROR :

Example: ON ERROR GOTO do.err

The ON ERROR statement is used to setup a routine that can be
used when an error occurs. When an error occurs, execution will be
transferred to the label that was specified. The second syntax turns
off error trapping. Whenever you link to another segment you must
set up a new ON ERROR vector to a routine within that segment. If
you don't have a vector set up and an error occurs, the user will be
disconnected, an error message will be printed, and the system will go
to the ***RESTART S,M,Q prompt.

1.47   **ON NOCAR**

Syntax: ON NOCAR GOTO label
               ON NOCAR:

Example: ON NOCAR GOTO termin1

The ON NOCAR statement is used to setup a routine that can
be used when carrier is lost from a remote user. The first syntax sets
up the ON NOCAR vector, and the second clears it. When carrier
is lost, ACOS will then hang up the modem. It will then change the
current execution point to the label that was set up. Whenever you
link to another segment you must set up a new ON NOCAR vector to
a routine within that segment. If you don't have a vector set up and a
remote caller drops carrier, the system will just sit there until it times
out.

1.48   **OPEN**

Syntax: OPEN # device,filename

Example: OPEN #1,"b:users"

The OPEN statement is used to make files ready to do i/o with a program. You open a disk file using either device channel 1 or 2, and all further references to that channel will access the file associated with it. When you are finished with the file, use the CLOSE command. This will free up the device channel for later use. If you try to use a channel that is already in use, or one besides 1 and 2, you will get a BAD DEVICE CHANNEL error. If the file you open does not exist, no error will be generated. If you try to read from the file, it will appear to be empty. Use the CREATE command to make a file.

1.49   **PDL**

Syntax: expression=PDL(number)

Example: print "paddle 1 is set at";PDL(1)

The PDL function is used to read one of the paddles on the system. You can read paddle zero through three. The number returned will be in the range 0-255. This command has no argument checking. Could trigger softswitches above paddle locations.

1.50   **PEEK**

Syntax: expression=PEEK(address)

Example: if peek(-16287)>127 print "button 1 is on"

The PEEK function is used to find the value of a byte in memory. ADDRESS is a 16-bit memory location that will be read and returned. The returned value will be in the range 0-255.

1.51 **POKE**

Syntax: POKE address,value

Example: POKE -16368,0

The POKE statement is used to assign a memory location a value of your choice. ADDRESS is a 16 bit memory location and VALUE is a number in the range Q-255.

1.52 **POP**

Syntax: POP

Example: POP

The POP statement is used in conjunction with the PUSH or GOSUB statement. When encountered, it will take the current "RETURN ADDRESS" from the table in memory and get rid of it. Though not used often, this statement is very handy when you need to exit from a routine that was GOSUB-ed without using a RETURN.

1.53 **POSITION**

Syntax: POSITION #device,number,number[,number]

Example: POSITION #1,128,un,70

The POSITION statement is used to position within random access files. The first argument is the disk device channel number that was used to open the file. The second field is the length of each record. The third field is the record number to be positioned to. The fourth optional field is the offset within the record that is to be positioned to.

1.54   **PRINT**

Syntax: PRINT [#device,] [expression]
                    [,expression] [;]

Example: PRINT "this is a test";PRINT a$,b$;
                    PRINT #1,"data",a\b$

   The PRINT statement is probably the most used statement in the entire ACOS language. With it, you can communicate information to the outside world. Its syntax is very flexible and all examples of it can not be shown here. The following is a list of legal arguments within the PRINT command:

   Control: ',' – The comma is used to separate expressions within the print statement and will be printed literally.

   Control: ';' – The semi-colon is also used to separate expressions. It will not be printed when encountered. If a semi-colon is the last character in the line, then the carriage return will be suppressed.

   Control: '\' – The backslash is used to generate a newline character. Using the backslash, there is no need to use a bunch of print:print... statements.

   Exprs: TEXT – Text must be contained within quotes and will be printed exactly as typed. Within quotes, you may have any special characters including return. Having an open quote with no closing quote can prove to be an interesting experience.

   Exprs: STRING – The content of the listed string will be printed. Nothing special applies.

   Exprs:NUMBER – The content on the listed number will be printed. Nothing special applies.

1.55   **PUBLIC**

Syntax :   PUBLIC label

Example: PUBLIC main

The PUBLIC statement is used to make a label within a program module available to other modules to link to. If you wish to link to another program module, and start execution at a some point other than the beginning of the module, you will need to make that point public. You can have a maximum of eight public labels within a program module.

1.56   **PUSH**

Syntax :   PUSH label

Example: PUSH main

The push statement is a sub-set of the GOSUB statement. It does not actually change the current point of execution, but places a return address in a table so that the next time a RETURN statement is encountered, control will return to this point. A POP statement will remove the last address added to the return table.

1.57   **RAM**

Syntax: RAM

Example: move ram,34 to ram2

The RAM function is really just a constant pointer. It just points to a free 64 bytes of memory that has been set aside for program use. This is a read-only function. No set check is performed. Using this function when not set may cause issues.

1.58   **RAM2**

Syntax: RAM2

Example: fill ram2,34,0

The RAM2 function is the same as the RAM function except that is points to a different 64 bytes that are available for program use. Generally this memory is used in conjunction with the READ, WRITE, FLAG, NIBBLE, and BYTE functions. This is a read-only function. No set check is performed.   Using this function when not set may cause issues.

1.59   **RANDOM**

Syntax: expression=RANDOM(number)

Example: print "from 1 to 10 -> "RANDOM(10)

The RANDOM function is used to generate a random within the range 0-number. A new random number will be generated every time the system goes to get input. If you take two random numbers in a row, they will always be the same. If you need more than one, use the RND$ string between them. This will do a temporary re-random.

1.60   **READ**

Syntax: READ #device,memloc,number

Example: READ #1,ram2,34

The READ statement is used to load data from a file into memory in its binary form without any processing or changing. The input does not have to come from a file. It can come from the editor or a message file. It is similar to on Apple DOS BLOAD command. This command has no address checking – could corrupt memory.

1.61 **READY**

Syntax: READY filename
            READY #MSG(number)

Example: READY "e:mail"; READY #msg(un)

The READY statement is used to make a message file ready for use. It is similar to an OPEN statement being used before a file is accessed. After a message file is made ready, all following references to MSG will be directed to that file. Once a message file has been made ready, it can also be used in its second syntax to ready a specific message within the file. This is generally used if further references to the file will use the device channel associated with the message base.

1.62 **RECALL**

Syntax: RECALL "fname"

Example: recall "b:variables"

The RECALL statement will reload in the variable set that was saved via a STORE command. The existing variables will be cleared, and the RECALLed ones will take their place.

1.63 **RESUME**

Syntax: RESUME

Example: if ERR=14 resume

The RESUME statement is used to continue program execution after an error occurs. If this statement is executed, and an error has not occurred, error trapping will be turned off, and an error will occur.

1.64   **RETURN**

Syntax: RETURN

Example: RETURN

The RETURN statement is used in conjunction with the PUSH or GOSUB statement. When encountered, program execution is halted at its current location and a new execution address is pulled from a table in memory. If no address is present, a RETURN WITHOUT GOSUB error will occur.

1.65   **REWIND**

Syntax: REWIND

Example: REWIND

The REWIND statement is used to change the file pointer block to its previous location. Generally this is used with the READY #msg(x):copy #7 statements to perform "re-read" tasking.

1.66   **RIGHT$**

Syntax: string=RIGHT$(string,length)

Example :   x$=RIGHT$(a$,2)

The RIGHT$ function is used to assign a portion of a source string to another string. It will take LENGTH number of characters from the RIGHT of the source string and assign them to the new string. This command has no argument checking. argument = argument mod 256

1.67   **RND$**

Syntax: char=RND$

Example: print "Random pass: "RND$;RND$;RND$

The RND$ function is used to generate random characters. Each time RND$ is accessed a new random character will be returned. BE WARNED: The random number is generated from timing how long a user takes to enter their input. This really is a pretty random number since it is based on the user's typing skill and speed. The only problem is that the random character generator can start repeating patterns after about 15-20 characters have been generated and before another input has taken place to "re-randomize" the number.

1.68   **SET**

Syntax: SET   string=memloc,number

Example: SET pa$=ram,8

The SET statement is another statement set up for the optimum management of memory. With SET, you can manually set up pointers for strings anywhere in memory. Along with the location of the string, you can also specify the length. Whenever the string is accessed, the text present at the memory locations will be returned. This command has no address checking – could corrupt memory or trigger softswitches.

1.69   **SETINT**

Syntax: SETINT (string 1 [,string 1...])
              SETINT ("")
              SETINT (number)

Example: SETINT("");SETINT(1);SETINT("A")

The SETINT command is used to setup 'Interrupt' keys. Once setup, the system will check for those keys whenever text is being displayed. If one of the keys are encountered, all further output will be suppressed until an input statement of some kind is encountered or the SETINT is reset. To reset the SETINT command, use the second syntax. If you wish to set the interrupt keys to those pre-defined by the ACOS CONFIG program, use the third syntax. SETINT(1) will set the interrupt key to the 'File Stop' character. SETINT(2) will set the interrupt keys to the 'File Stop' and 'File Next' characters.

1.70   **SIZE**

Syntax: expression=SIZE(device)

Example: open # 1,"a:testflle":print size(1)

The SIZE function will allow you to determine the size of a file on disk. The only prerequisite is that the file is open. The size will be returned in 256 byte block units. A file that returns a size of 5 is therefore approximately 1280 bytes. Doesn't check for 0.

1.71   **STORE**

Syntax: STORE "fname"

Example: store "b:variables"

The STORE command will save the values of all the variables (both numerical and strings) onto a disk file. This is useful if another segment will be used that may have conflicting variable names.

1.72   **STR$**

Syntax: string=STRS(number)

Example: a$=STR$(123)

The STR$ function is used to change a number into a string. Once turned into a string, the number cannot be used in any mathematical operation. To convert the string back to a number, use the VAL function.

1.73   **TEXT**

Syntax: TEXT

Example: TEXT

The TEXT statement is used to reset the screen size and clear the screen.

1.74   **TIME$**

Syntax: string=TIMES

Example: print "The time is: "TIME$

The TIME$ function is used to get the current time from your clock. If your system is equipped with a clock, the time will be returned in a "HH:MM:SS XM" type of format. If your clock is in 24 hour configuration then it will be returned in "HH:MM:SS" format.

1.75   **TONE**

Syntax: TONE(nvar1,nvar2,[nvar3])

Example: TONE (50,60,100)

The TONE command will generate sound from the local speaker. If you only use the first two arguments (as the pitch and duration) it will give true sound. If using the third argument, the first two become pitch and offset. The third then becomes the duration. This command has no argument checking. argument = argument mod 256

1.76   **UPDATE**

Syntax: UPDATE

Example: msg(a)=0:kill #msg(a):update

The UPDATE statement is used to change the bit-map and directory of a message file. This is to reflect changes made to the messages themselves. For example, when a message is deleted, UPDATE will de-allocate its space. The next time a message is posted the empty space will be used.

1.77   **USE**

Syntax: USE fname [,parms(,parms...)]

Example: USE "b:xdos",i$

The USE statement is used to access a 4K or smaller routine from a disk file that is external to the language. These 'external files' are loaded in and executed. The USE command will get parameters from the continuation of the line after the filename argument.

1.78   **VAL**

Syntax: nexprs=VAL(svar)

Example: z=val(i$)

The VAL statement is used to find the numerical value of a string. The VAL statement is used when you have a string containing a number. This command has no limit checking. Overflow is ignored, and large numbers will be reduced to -32768 to 32767.

1.79   **WHEN$**

Syntax: WHEN$=memloc
               sexprs=WHEN$
               WHEN$=svar

Example: when$=a$:a$=when$

The WHEN$ statement is a date compression scheme. The first syntax points WHEN$ to two free bytes in memory. When the WHEN$ function is used, two bytes will be retrieved from memory and will be translated into a "MM/DD/YY" format. When you assign WHEN$ a value, the current date will be read and changed into a two byte compressed format and saved to the current memory pointer. This command has no address checking – could corrupt memory or trigger softswitches.;

1.80   **WIDTH**

Syntax: nexprs=WIDTH(nvar)

Example   a=width(0)

In the first syntax, WIDTH(x) (where x is 1-4) will return the 4 most commonly used video widths. WIDTH(0) will return the number of the width (1-4) that should be used as a default.

1.81   **WRITE**

Syntax: WRITE #dev,memloc,nvar

Example: write #1,ram,34

The WRITE statement is used to write binary data from memory to one of ACOS's device channels. The only channel that cannot be used is #7. The second argument is the memory location from which ACOS will write. The third is the number of bytes to write. This command has no address checking – could trigger softswitches.

Device Specifiers

#0:   Local and remote consoles (default)

#1:   Disk file #1

#2:   Disk file #2

#3:   Local console only

#4:   Remote console only (modem)

#5:   Printer

#6:   Message file – read/write

#7:   Message file – read only

#8:   Editor

#9:   Inverse "top of screen" display

#10:   Internal 128 byte RAM area
        (this space is NOT the same as RAM or RAM2)

Default Drive Specifiers

A: Program drive

B: System drive

C: General Files drive

D: Download drive

E: Upload drive

F: Bulletin drive

G: Mail drive

H: - L: User expansion

Error Messages

1: STARTING MODULE NOT FOUND

ACOS was unable to locate the starting program module. By default, this file is named "LOGON.SEG", but may be changed via the ACOS loader program.

2: MODULE TOO LARGE

The compiled segment is too large to be loaded into memory. If this error occurs, try breaking the segment into several smaller ones.

3: LABEL NOT FOUND

The ACOS compiler could not find a label that was referenced in the program.

4: SYMBOL TABLE FULL

There are too many labels in the symbol table. ACOS will only allow a maximum of 255 labels per segment.

5: SYNTAX ERROR

Missing parenthesis in a line, misspelling of a keyword, misuse of punctuation, etc.

6: MISSING SYMBOL

There was no label following a GOTO, GOSUB, or a PUSH.

7: UNDEFINED LABEL

This occurs when a segment is being executed and reference is made to a label that cannot be found.

8: MISSING DATA

Occurs when a program statement has no valid argument. For example, X=clock() is missing data because there is no valid number between the parenthesis.

9: TYPE MISMATCH

A string variable was used when a numeric variable was required. A numeric variable was used when a string variable was required. A string variable was compared to a numeric variable.

10: OVERFLOW > 32767

ACOS cannot handle numbers < -32767 or > 32767.

11: DIVISION BY ZERO

Dividing by zero is always an error.

12: STRING TOO LONG

An attempt was mode to create a string larger then 255 characters.

13: GOSUB STACK FULL

ACOS will not allow nesting of more than 16 GOSUBS.

14: RETURN WITHOUT GOSUB

A RETURN or POP statement was encountered without a corresponding GOSUB or PUSH being executed.

15: BAD DEVICE NUMBER

A device was accessed that was not OPEN or READY, or the device does not exist.

16: ILLEGAL FILENAME

The syntax of the filename is illegal or an attempt is made to use a disk channel that is already OPEN.

17: FOR STACK FULL

ACOS will not allow you to nest more than 16 FOR statements.

18: NEXT WITHOUT FOR

A NEXT statement was encountered without a corresponding FOR statement being executed.

19: LINK LABEL NOT FOUND

An attempt to LINK into a segment at a label that is either not public or does not exist.

20: MESSAGE FILE NOT FOUND

The message tile that was accessed with the READY statement does not exist.

21: END OF PROGRAM

An END statement has been encountered, or ACOS has reached the end of a program.

22: BAD DRIVE SPECIFIER

An attempt was made to access a drive or pathname that does not exist.

23: UNABLE TO LOAD EXTERNAL

ACOS was unable to find an external module.

24: UNCLOSED QUOTE AT EOF

At the end of compiling the program, a quote (" or ') was still open. This indicates that some string statement was started, but not finished.

25: ARGUMENT OUT OF RANGE

Value provided to a command is not valid for the command

26: INVALID ADDRESS

The address provided to BYTE, NIBBLE, FLAG or CALL is unavailable to ACOS.

Recovering from a system crash

Recovering From a System Crash

In the unlikely event of a system crash, there are some steps you should follow to help you diagnose and correct the problem. Generally, if you don't fix the problem, it isn't going to go away. Of course, the best protection is prevention. Having a backup is always easier than re-writing data and thinking up changes all over again.

Keeping a regular schedule of backups is a good form of preventive maintenance. The major files that you need to backup include the DATA and USERS files, the MAIL file and each of the Bx bulletin files. Also, if you make mods to your system, keep a backup of the segments that you change. With the above data backed up, recovering from a system crash need not be a painful experience.

If you come home and find that your system is displaying the "RESTART" prompt, an error has taken place. The first thing to do is analyze what you see on the screen. What were the last commands that took place before the system crashed? Try and duplicate the problem. If a problem can be duplicated, it can be eliminated. To find out exactly where in the code a program is crashing, turn on the ACOS trace mode. Next, cause the error to happen. When it takes place, you will be able to see where in the code the error is.

If you are unable to locate the error, get a listing of the original program as it came to you and compare the code, line by line. Chances are you will find your error this way. If you are sure that the code is the original code, and you have made no changes to it, submit a bug report through the *GBBS Pro* source code website and we will endeavor to find a solution.

ACOS Memory Map

```
$C000 +--------------------------+     $5100 +--------------------------+
      |        PRODOS MLI        |           |   ACOS PROGRAM KERNEL    |
$BF00 +--------------------------+     $1200 +--------------------------+
      |   MSG FILE DATA BUFFER   |           |       MODEM DRIVER       |
$BB00 +--------------------------+     $0E00 +--------------------------+
      |  MSG FILE DIRECTORY BLK  |           |       CLOCK DRIVER       |
$B900 +--------------------------+     $0D00 +--------------------------+
      |    MSG FILE BLOCK BUF 2  |           |      PRINTER DRIVER      |
$B880 +--------------------------+     $0C00 +--------------------------+
      |    MSG FILE BLOCK BUF 1  |           |       VIDEO DRIVER       |
$B800 +--------------------------+     $0900 +--------------------------+
      |    MESSAGE FILE BITMAP   |           |   DRIVE SPECS/ACOS DATA  |
$B780 +--------------------------+     $0800 +--------------------------+
      |     TYPE AHEAD BUFFER    |           |       TEXT PAGE 1        |
$B700 +--------------------------+     $0400 +--------------------------+
      |         RAMDRIVE         |           |   PRODOS/MONITOR DATA    |
$B680 +--------------------------+     $03D0 +--------------------------+
      |     INTERRUPT FLAGS      |           |    ACOS ENTRY POINTS     |
$B600 +--------------------------+     $0380 +--------------------------+
      |      FILE 1 BUFFER       |           |       RAM2 BUFFER        |
$B200 +--------------------------+     $0340 +--------------------------+
      |      FILE 2 BUFFER       |           |        RAM BUFFER        |
$AE00 +--------------------------+     $0300 +--------------------------+
      |     EDITOR/USE BUFFER    |           |    LINE INPUT BUFFER     |
$9E00 +--------------------------+     $0200 +--------------------------+
      |                          |           |       6502 STACK         |
      |    SEGMENT/VARIABLES     |     $0100 +--------------------------+
      |                          |           |        ZERO PAGE         |
$5100 +--------------------------+     $0000 +--------------------------+
```

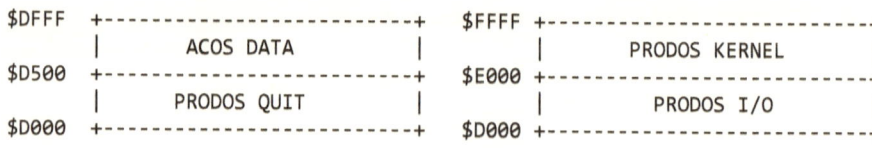

16K Card Bank 1   ## 16K Card Bank 2

```
$DFFF +--------------------------+     $FFFF +--------------------------+
      |        ACOS DATA         |           |      PRODOS KERNEL       |
$D500 +--------------------------+     $E000 +--------------------------+
      |       PRODOS QUIT        |           |        PRODOS I/O        |
$D000 +--------------------------+     $D000 +--------------------------+
```

CHAPTER 6

Modifying the System

Modifying GBBS Pro

One of the most important aspects of *GBBS Pro* is that the system is easy to modify. It provides the flexibility to fit many different applications. Providing this flexibility was the reason for the development of ACOS and the subsequent design of the bulletin board.

Every attempt has been made to make *GBBS Pro* as versatile and as flexible as its *GBBS II* predecessor. Even though you cannot move code over directly from the older *GBBS II* system, *GBBS Pro* was designed so that the ideas can still be implemented in the same ways. Most of the commonly used routines from *GBBS II* are present in some form within *GBBS Pro*. In many cases, you will probably find that your mods become easier to make in ACOS.

Modifying the text of the system is really very easy. Just load the segment that contains the text you wish to edit into a word/text processor of your choice. From there, it is just a matter of editing. The only rule you must observe is to keep text in quotes that started that in quotes. That is, if the original text had quotes around it, make sure you do not remove them.

Third party extensions are a great way to expand the capabilities of *GBBS Pro*. Popular choices include *Super Total Access Control* (*SuperTAC*) or *ExFer* add support for YMODEM and ZMODEM transfer protocols.

Board Modifications

The following modifications are provided merely as a guide and as examples to help you on your way to making your own mods. Most of the following mods are fairly simple, and some are more or less useless. Just keep in mind that the point is to try and illustrate how to modify your system.

Whenever reference is made below to a segment of code, an approximate point from a known label in the code will be given. Just find this label within the segment, and that will be where the change should go. Again, to modify a segment, just load it into a word/text processor and do the editing.

Referencing a Bulletin Board via a Command

In the old days of *GBBS II*, the common way to access different bulletin boards was to have different commands from the main command prompt. Some people still like this method and may wish to use it. To reference a specific bulletin board from the command section, you just do the following:

1. Load MAIN.SEG.S into a text editor.

2. You will want to place the line to access the board after the MAIN label in one of the two groups of commands. If placed in the first group, it will be available to all users. If placed in the second group, it will be available to verified users only. The person's security will also be checked when they actually enter the board. An example line would look like:

   ```
   IF I$="6502" THEN BB=3:A$="BULLETINS":GOTO LINK.MSG
   ```

   In this particular case, the board accessed would be Board 3. Just assign the board number to BB and set A$ equal to the word "BULLETINS". Then go to the LINK.MSG routine as done above. That is all you need to do.

3. Save MAIN.SEG.S back to disk.

Adding Another Download Section

1. Use your text/word processor to create a file called "Dxx" where XX is the section number you want to add. Your first section is section one, you second would be two, and so on. We will use section two for this example.

2. On the first line of this file, enter the number of files that will be in the download section. You can then list all the files in any format that you like. In this section, we will have three files:

   ```
   3 (the number of entries on the first line)
   01 023 BACH SONGS (the 01 is the file number)
   02 006 DISK COPY 48K (006 is the optional length)
   03 023 SUPER-EDIT
   ```

3. After you have created and saved the file "D2", load in the segment "MAIN.SEG.S".

4. We now need to add a line to the code to access the new section of files. We will assume that the new download section files are on "C:" with the first section. You can now add the line anywhere within the group of IF-THENs following the label MAIN1.

   ```
   IF (I$="X2") AND FLAG(2) A$="C:D2":GOTO DOWNLOAD
   ```

   First, we check for the command "X2". If that was the command typed, we check to see if security flag two is set. If not, the caller will not be able to access this section. If the AND FLAG(2) argument had been omitted, any verified user would have been able to access the section. We then set A$ equal to the name of the base file (D2), adding on a drive specifier so the system knows where to find the file. Last, we just execute the download routine.

5. Save MAIN.SEG.S back to disk.

Adding Feedback to a User

1. Load MAIN.SEG.S into a text editor.

2. Imagine that you have an on-line RPG game going on and you
   would like the players to have an easy way to send their comments
   to the Dungeon Master. You are not the DM, another user is, so
   they cannot use feedback. You need to have some way to add
   another feedback section that can send the mail to your DM.

   For this example, your DM's user number is 17. You want
all feedback to be headed with the title "COMMENTS FROM A
PLAYER". To add a feedback section like this, you would have to add
some code after the label MAIN1 like:

```
IF (I$="DM") AND FLAG(3) GOTO FEED.DM
```

This first line is just to dispatch program control to another routine
in the program called FEED.DM. We have restricted its use to those
users with security flag three set. We then locate a place within the
segment that we want to add our actual mod at. To do a feedback
section, it would make sense to add it after the currently existing
feedback to Sysop routine.

```
; Feedback to the DM

FEED.DM
 PRINT \"A QUESTION TO THE DM"
 GOSUB EDITOR:IF NOT EDIT(2) RETURN
 H$= " COMMENTS FROM A PLAYER":D=17
 PRINT  \"WAIT..";:A$="WR.LETTER"
 GOSUB LINK.MSG:PRINT ".FEEDBACK SAVED"
 RETURN
```

The first line with the semicolon is merely a comment for your
own records. It will help you to remember what the routine is for. The
routine works as follows:

ACOS first prints an intro to the user. Next, it enters the editor and gets their comments. The code then checks to see if they aborted from the editor (NOT EDIT(2)). If they did, the segment just returns. Otherwise, you set H$ to the header you want posted on the letter. D is then set to the user number of the user to get the letter. The message WAIT.. is displayed and the letter is sent. There is then a confirmation message and the routine returns.

3. Save MAIN.SEG.S back to disk.

Adding Another Command Section

1. Load MAIN.SEG.S into a text editor.

2. You may find at some time that you wish to add another complete command section in addition to the one you already have. Taking the RPG game as a scenario, you might want to have a completely different command section, which includes commands to access the board, send feedback to the DM, and have a general files section with specific information. In any case, in this example you will enter a new command section that includes commands to access the board, and terminate the system. Again, you can add as many commands as you like.

Adding the new section is not complicated at all. To do this you just locate a place within the segment where you wish to add the new lines. First though, you must add a line to the current command section to access this new one. Placing the line after the MAIN1 label, it might look like:

```
IF I$="RPG" GOTO RPG
```

You will be using RPG as a label to reference our code by. You just need to locate a spot within the segment and insert a few lines. After the label MAIN2 would probably be a good spot. You then add some lines such as:

```
RPG
 INPUT \"RPG COMMAND (?=HELP):" I$:PUSH RPG
 IF I$="B":BB=2:A$="BULLETINS":GOTO LINK.MSG
 IF I$="T" GOTO TERMINATE
 IF I$<>"?" PRINT \"ILLEGAL COMMAND":RETURN
 SETINT(1):PRINT \$$\'
 ################################
 #       PUT YOUR MENU HERE        #
 ################################
 ';:RETURN
```

The design of the section is really very simple. You start by giving the user a prompt and getting their command. The PUSH RPG is what allows the system to know where to return to once each command is complete. You then just check for each command. Finally, you check to see if they wanted help (?). If not, they typed in an illegal command. Otherwise, the help menu will be displayed. You help file can say whatever you wish.

3. Save MAIN.SEG.S back to disk.

Adding Another General Files Section

1. Load MAIN.SEG.S into a text editor.

2. Adding another general files section is not difficult. It is just a matter of adding a line to access the new section. Again, add the line somewhere after the MAIN1 label.

   ```
   IF I$="G2" AND FLAG(2):A$="C:G2":GOTO GENERAL
   ```

   It first checks to see if the user entered the command "G2". If they did, then it checks to see if they have the proper security clearance. If so, then it sets A$ equal to the base file name, and goes to the general files routine.

3. Save MAIN.SEG.S back to disk.

4. At this point, the system will access another general files section. but something still needs to be put in it. Edit a file called "G2" on

"C:". On the first line, put the number of general files that will be in that section as with download. The rest of the file may be "free-form" for you to make look any way to like. For example:

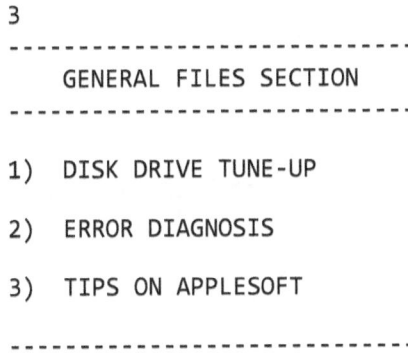

```
3
------------------------------
        GENERAL FILES SECTION
------------------------------

1)  DISK DRIVE TUNE-UP

2)  ERROR DIAGNOSIS

3)  TIPS ON APPLESOFT

------------------------------
```

Of course, you can change the style to fit your tastes. The main point is that the first line contain the number of entries that will be available.

Running the System Turnkey

1. To run your system turnkey, you must first set up your system so that the boot disk is always on-line. No disk swapping must take place when the system boots up.

2. Enter the following program in BASIC:

```
10 POKE 1,1:POKE 2,2
20 ?CHR$(4)"-ACOS"
```

3. Save the program to your BOOT disk. Save it under the name STARTUP.

4. When the system is booted, the above program will be loaded into memory and run. The program does two POKEs that tell ACOS not to wait for any input. It then runs ACOS which will in return, run the system.

Main Routines

TERMINATE – The user is given one chance to abort. If they do not, then the connection will be broken and users and data files will be written back to disk.

CHAT – This routine will page the Sysop up to three times. After the third time, the message "SYSOP NOT AVAILABLE" will be given. After the sixth time the user will be logged off. Also, the tone will be different for verified and privileged users.

SHOW.STAT – This routine will display to the user all their personal stats. It will also show records 1 through 34 of the DATA2 file that correspond to the security flags that the user has set.

USERLIST – This routine will display the list of users. As Sysop you can also display their passwords and time limits.

FEEDBACK – This routine allows the user to send feedback to the Sysop's mailbox.

GENERAL – This is the general files section. Upon entry, A$ needs to be set to the base filename for the general files. It must also contain a drive specifier.

DISPLAY – The display section allows a user to change certain system parameters, including video width, nulls, paging, phone number display, and backspace status. No entry variables needed.

GETPASS – For guest users, this routine will give them the option of going and getting a regular password.

SETPASS – For verified users, this routine will let them change their password (PAS).

VOTING – This routine handles all the system voting. A$ must be set to the base voting file and include a drive specifier: A$="B:V2":GOTO VOTING is a good example of voting access.

FORCE – This is a sub-part of the VOTING routine. This routine will allow you to make all system users vote on a certain section. Just assign A$ the name of the voting file and GOSUB FORCE at the beginning of the MAIN.SEG.S segment. If the user has not voted, then they will be forced to. If they have, the routine will just return.

LINK.MSG – This is the routine that is used to change control to one of the four message segment routines: (BULLETINS, SEND MAIL, READ MAIL, WRITE MAIL). To use it, just set A$ to the name of the routine to be called (BULLETINS, RD.MAIL, SD.MAIL, WR.LETTER) and GOSUB LINK.MSG. For WR.LETTER, control of the destination user for the private message is handled by the variable D. You must also have SB$ set to the subject. The optional header is set in H$, and if it's empty then no header is added to the message.

BULLETINS – This must be accessed through the LINK.MSG routine. You can set BB before entering bulletins to set the currently loaded bulletin board to that board number.

EDITOR – This is just the system editor. If you GOSUB EDITOR, the user will be placed in the editor and will be able to enter a message.

SHOW.FILE – This routine will display any file to the user. The filename must be in F$ and may optionally contain a drive specifier. If the user has the paging option on, it will take effect here.

Variable Listing

There are many variables used within the shells that make up *GBBS Pro*. The names of the variables and their uses:

A   General purpose variable. Used all over.

A$ General purpose. Also used to assign names for routines such as voting, general files, and download.

A1   Command attempt counter.

A1$ User's first name.

A2$ User's last name.

A3$ User's full name (lowercase)

A4$ User's city.

A5$ User's state.

AB   Bulletin board count.

B   General purpose variable. Used all over.

B$ Name/file name matching.

B1   Flag variable. Used in bulletins to show whether user has access to a board or not.

B2   Flag variable. Used in bulletins to show whether user has write access to a board.

B3   Scratch variable used with B1.

B4   Scratch variable used with B2.

B5   Save for BB.

BB   Current board number.

BF$ Board filename.

BL   Board number, set but never read.

BN$ Current board name.

BP   Number of bulletins the user has posted.

BS   Auxillary Sysop number for bulletin boards.

BS$ Auxillary Sysop name for bulletin boards.

C   General purpose variable.

C$ Name matching.

C1   System calls times 10000.

C2   System calls low byte. Every time this variable gets to 10000 it
          is reset to zero and C1 in incremented by 1.

CH   Chat try count.

CM$ Date and time the connection was made.

CN$ Call number text.

CT   Total number of calls today.

CT$ Date string for the caller today count.

D   Destination user id of electronic mail being sent.

D$ Used for city in user list.

D1$ Aux first name field.

D2$ Aux last name field.

D3$ Aux full name field.

D4$ Aux city field.

D5$ Aux state field.

DA$ Current date.

DL   Number of downloads the user has taken.

E$ Used for state in user list.

F$ Filename to be displayed when the file print routine is used.
          Also used internally for filenames within some routines.

FL   Profanity filter location.

FR$ From name.

FV   Force the user to vote: 0 = Don't force them. 1 = Force them.

H$ Header (optional).

I$ Current input.

KB   Bulletin to be killed when the auto-kill limit has been reached.

KL   Auto-kill limit for the current bulletin board.

L   General purpose loop counter.

LC$ Date of the last call of the user.

LG   Log file use flag: 0 = Don't save it. 1 = Save to disk.

LR   Last bulletin read number for a user. Updated each time a bulletin is read and saved to the user file.

LU$ Name of the last user.

M$ Scan for text.

MA   Mail status. 0 = Mail either non-existent or unread. 1 = Mail read and ready to be deleted.

MB   Maximum number of bulletins on the current board.

MD$ Mail divider string. Must be 39 characters.

ME   Used in bulletin marking.

MN   Next bulletin number to be allocated.

MS   Bulletins marked.

N   Cursor move count for erasing.

N$ Next bulletin text.

NB   New bulletin number. Set once from LR when the user logs on.

NN   New bulletin number. Set every time a user changes boards.

NU   Number of records in the user file.

OB   Old bulletin board number.

PA$ Current user's password. (8 characters)

PF   Profanity filter temporary setup.

PH$ Current user's phone number. (12 characters)

R$ Message sent/forwarded text.

S   Used for displaying messages.

S$ Message "Ctrl-S stop/start Spacebar to Exit"

SB$ Mail/message subject.

SC$ Screen clear character.

SN$ System name.

SV$ Sysop secondary password.

SYS$ Name of the Sysop.

T$ Temporary used in message scan.

TC   Times called.

TI$ To name.

TM   Total messages.

TN   To user number.

UL   Number of uploads the user has given.

UN   Current user number.

WM   Welcome message number.

X   General purpose. Used all over.

X$ Portion of day (morning, afternoon, evening)

Y   General purpose. Used all over.

Z   General purpose. Used all over.

Z$ Temporary for formatting user baud rate.

ZX   Message move destination board.

ZZ   Next/previous message direction.

The following functions (Flag, Nibble, Byte) are very similar to variables in their operation. As a result, the definitions of these functions has been placed with the variables.

Flags

FLAG(0)   Set if user is a Guest.

FLAG(1)   Set if user is Verified.

FLAG(2)   Set if user is Privileged.

FLAG(3)
  to   Left for user security expansion.
FLAG(33)

FLAG(34)   Set if user is Sysop.

FLAG(35)   Set if paging mode on.

FLAG(36)   Set if anonymous mode on.

FLAG(37)   Set if profanity filter on.

FLAG(38)   Used by Anonymous Posting routines.

FLAG(39)   Left for option expansion.

Nibbles

NIBBLE(0)   Bits 3,2 are the backspace mode for the user. Bits 1,0 are the user's video width (based on a lookup table).

NIBBLE(1)   High byte of Calls made.

NIBBLE(2)   High byte of Bulletins posted.

NIBBLE(3)   High byte of Downloads.

NIBBLE(4)   High byte of Uploads.

NIBBLE(5)   User's time limit (10 min. units).

NIBBLE(6)   Number of calls made today.

NIBBLE(7)
   to   Future use and user expansion.
NIBBLE(19)

Bytes

BYTE(0)   User's null print value.

BYTE(1)   Low byte of Calls made.

BYTE(2)   Low byte of Bulletins posted.

BYTE(3)   Low byte of Downloads.

BYTE(4)   Low byte of Uploads.

BYTE(5)   Low byte of new message number.

BYTE(6)   High byte of new message number.

BYTE(7)
   to   Future use and user expansion.
BYTE(19)

Disk File Info

There are several text files on disk that may be of interest to the user. Both the files "DATA" and "DATA1" can be easily changed using any text editor or the system editor. The files "DATA2" and "USERS" are both random access and therefore can only be changed by special code written for them.

Description of the File: DATA

Line 1:   calls * 10000, calls mod 10000, calls today, calls today date, the real date.

Line 2:   number of users, new message number, welcome message number, total number of messages on system.

Line 3:   name of the last user to call.

Description of the File: DATA1

Line 1:   Name of the system

Line 2:   Name of the sysop

Line 3:   Secondary sysop password

Line 4:   Mail divider (39 "-"'s)

Line 5:   "spacebar to exit" message

Line 6:   "N for next bulletin" message

Line 7:   Log status 0/1; 1 = Log saved, Forced voting 0/1; 1 = Forced voting enabled

Description of the File: DATA2

First half of file has 32 byte records

+0:   Message for Security Level 0 (guest)

+32:   Message for Security Level 1 (normal)

+64:   Message for Security Level 2 (edit)

+96:   Message for Security Level 3

+128:   Message for Security Level 4
  to
+1088:   Message for Security Level 34 (Sysop)

+1120:   Number of Bulletin Boards in use

Second half of file has 128 byte records

+1152:   Bulletin Board 1 parameters

+1280:   Bulletin Board 2 parameters

+1408:   Bulletin Board 3 parameters...

Bulletin Board Parameters:

Line 1: Board name

Line 2: Filename

Line 3: Access flag, Write flag

Line 4: Aux Sysop number, aux Sysop name

Line 5: Max bulletins, Auto-kill limit, Bulletin to kill

Description for the File: USERS

File has 128 bytes records

+0:   Empty record

+128:   User record #1 (Sysop)

+256:   User record #2

+384:   User record #3

User Record Parameters:

Line 1: First name, last name

Line 2: Full name (upper/lowercase)

Line 3: Calling from (city, state)

Binary data at +70 byte offset into record

+70:   8 byte ASCII password

+78:   12 byte ASCII phone number

+00:   2 byte last called date in ProDOS format

+92:   5 bytes have all 40 user flags

+97:   10 bytes have all 19 nibble orgs

+107:   20 bytes has all 19 byte orgs

Assembly Language Info

The following text assumes that the reader has a good working knowledge of assembly language. All addresses and data are given in hexadecimal. Every attempt will be made to keep the listed locations the same in later versions, but they may change without notice.

External Modules

To help make ACOS more flexible, it has been equipped with the ability to use "external files". These are small (under 4K) machine language routines that are loaded into memory and then executed to perform special extended functions. The normal system includes three external modules: one for uploads, another for downloads, and lastly one for DOS commands. These files are stored as binary files. These files are loaded into ACOS's editor buffer. This buffer is located $9e00. The Language Card is always enabled so no special manipulation of soft-switches is needed.

From ACOS, an external module is accessed via the "USE" command. As a basic example, the following will show how the "X.DN" file is used in conjunction with the download section in both ACOS and machine language environments.

```
Z=1:F$="C:TESTFILE":USE "B:X.DN",Z,F$
```

In the above case, the external module "X.DN" is to be used to download the file "TESTFILE" from the drive "C:" using transfer method 2. First, the binary code for "X.DN" is loaded into memory in the editor buffer. Transfer then passes to the start of the buffer. An example group of code that would set up the file name and get the transfer method is:

```
$9E00: JSR GOBCOM ;gobble the comma
$9E03: JSR INPNUM ;get transfer type
$9E06: STX XFERTYP ;save transfer type
$9E09: JSR GOBCOM ;gobble comma after type
$9E0C: JSR MOVNAME ;setup filename to xfer
   .
   .   ;actual code here
   .
$9E0F: JSR OPEN ;the file can be opened
   .
   .   ;more code goes here
   .
$xxxx: RTS ;just return once done
```

Zero Page Locations

$04: .i.PRGPTR;   Pointer to the current address within the segment from where the program is being executed. If you change this address, it has the same effect as issuing a GOTO in ACOS.

$0C: .i.CMD;   This is the current token that is being executed by ACOS.

$22: .i.WNDTOP;   Top line of text window.

$23: .i.WNDBTM;   Bottom line of text window.

$24: .i.CH;   Current horizontal "cursor" position. This location controls where the next character will be placed on the screen (via a call to VIDCOUT). The cursor is created by the input routine.

$25: .i.CV;   Current vertical cursor location.

$32: .i.INVFLG;   Inverse mode Off/On. High-bit clear sets inverse off.

$61: .i.LOGOFF;   ACOS has detected a loss of carrier and disconnected the phone. Whatever routines are executing should quit and return. The high-bit will be set once ACOS disconnects the user.

$63: .i.TYPIN;   Index for the input side of the system input buffer. It is in the range G-127.

$64: .i.TYPOUT;   Index for the output side of the input buffer. Data from this side goes to the normal input routines. By setting both $63 and $64 to zero, you can clear the input buffer.

$81: .i.VNAME;   Two-byte name of the current variable ACOS is using. The variable type can be determined by checking the high-bit of $81. If the high-bit is clear, the variable is numeric. If the high-bit is set, the variable is a string.

$83: VPTR Pointer to the current variables record. If the variable is numeric, then its record will contain its value in 16-bit signed integer format. If the variable is a string the record will contain a 16-bit pointer to the data, and the length of the string following the pointer. Each record is actually 6 bytes long: bytes 0,1 are the name, 2,3,4 are the value or a pointer, 5 is currently not used.

$C9: Random number seed. Every time ACOS is waiting for an input, it continuously changes this seed location.

Handy Sub-Routines

$380: GETBYT Get the next byte from the segment in memory. It will also advance the program pointer.

$383: CHKBYT Get the next byte from the segment in memory without moving the pointer. This is generally used to check for optional parameters.

$386: GOBCOM When you want to "gobble" a command from the program. If called and the next byte is not a comma, then a syntax error and a restart condition will be generated.

$389: INPNUM Input a number as text or a junction, performing the needed math to get the result. The number is returned as a 16-bit signed integer in A & X.

$38C: INPSTR Input a string. Upon return, A & X will point to the memory location of the string and Y will contain its length. It also sets up the zero page locations VNAME & VPTR.

$38F: MOVNAME Move a filename into ACOS's internal filename buffer. This call must be used prior to calling OPEN.

$392: BADERR   ACOS error handler. To use it, load X with the
                   error message number and call the routine. It
                   will display the message and go into the system
                   restart condition.

$395: SETIVEC   Allow the user to set the input device to any one
                   of the device channels. To use this routine, load
                   Y with the channel number and call the routine.

$398: GET   Poll the user for an input character. On return,
                   A is set to zero if no data was present, or it will
                   contain the data with the high-bit clear.

$39B: GETCHR   Checks for and returns a character from the
                   type ahead buffer. It returns the same as GET.
                   Generally, in an input routine. GETCHR is
                   called first. If no data is present, GET is called
                   until data is found.

$39E: INPLN   Input a line of data from the console/modem.
                   The input will be placed at $200. The input will
                   be terminated by a CR ($0D). The length of the
                   input will also be returned in Y.

$3A1: SETOVEC   Allow the user to set the output device to any
                   of the device channels. To use this routine, set
                   Y with the device channel number and call the
                   routine.

$3A4: COUT   Standard character output routine. Along with
                   outputting the character in A, it also handles the
                   type ahead buffer.

$3A7: DECOUT   Display the contents of A & X as an integer
                   from -32767 to 32768.

$3AA: CREATE   Create a blank file on disk. You must call
                   MOVNAME prior to calling CREATE.

$3AD: OPEN   Open a file so that it can be read from and
                  written to. You must call MOVNAME prior
                  to calling OPEN. Carry will be set if an error
                  occurred.

$3B0: CLOSE   Close the open file. Only one file may be open
                  at a time.

$3B3: RDBYTE   Get a byte from the current open file. If no data
                  is present, A will be zero and carry set.

$3B6: WRBYTE   Value of A will be written to the current open
                  file.

$3B9: RDBLK   Read one or more blocks from on open file.
                  To call this routine, A & X should point to the
                  destination of the data. Y should contain the
                  number of 128 byte blocks to read. Carry set
                  indicates end of data.

$3BC: WRBLK   Write one or more blocks of data to the open
                  file. To call this routine, A & X should point to
                  the source of the data and Y should contain the
                  number of 128 byte blocks to write.

$3BF: RDLINE   Special high-speed routine for reading a line
                  (0-254 characters terminated by a CR ($D)) of
                  text into the input line buffer at $200. Carry set
                  indicates end of data.

$3C2: GETMRK   Get the data pointer for the open file. The mark
                  will be returned in Y, A, X, 'Y' is the high byte,
                  'A' is the middle byte, and 'X' is the low byte.

$3C5: SETMRK   Set the data pointer for the open file. Upon entry
                  Y must contain the high byte, A the middle byte,
                  and X the low byte of the mark address.

Device Addresses

Video Driver starts at $900

$900: VIDINIT   Initialize the local video.

$903: VIDCLS   Clear the screen.

$906: VIDCOUT   Display character in A on the screen at the current cursor location ($24,$25).

$909: VIDSCRL   Scroll the screen one line.

$90C: VIDBAN   Scroll the character in A across the 24th line.

$90F: VIDLST   Clear the last line of the video display.

$912: VIDRDST   Initialize the read-key routine.

$915: VIDRDKY   Blinks cursor.

$918: VIDRDFN   Finish read-key routine.

$91B: VIDWND   Display top of screen window.

$91E: VIDRD   Read the contents of video line X into $280. Length of line in Y.

$921: VIDKEY   Read local keyboard. BMI if data in A and the high-bit will be set.

$924: VIDPOS   Position on the screen to X,Y.

Printer Driver starts at $C00

$C00: PRSLOT   Slot of the printer * 16.

$C01: PRINIT   Initialize the printer.

$C04: PRCOUT   Print the character in A.

$C07: PRCLEAR   Clear the printer buffer. Not currently implemented in any driver.

Clock Driver starts at $D00

$D00: CLKSLOT   Slot of the clock * 16.

$D01: CLKMODE   Clock driver 12/24 hour mode flag. If high bit is set, time will be returned in 12-hour format. If the high bit is clear, time will be returned in 24-hour format.

$D02: GETDATE   Gets the current date in 2-byte form. It is returned in A & X; A=YYYYYYYM X=MMMDDDDD.

$D05: GETTIME   Returns the current time in the form "HH:MM:SS XM". A & X are returned pointing to the string.

$008: SETDATE   Sets the current date from an 8 character string in the format "MM/DD/YY". Upon entry, A & X point to the new date string.

Modem Driver starts at $E00

$E00: MDMSLOT   Slot of the modem * 16.

$E01: TRANRCV   Current "mode" of the program. If the high-bit is clear, the program is in output mode. If high-bit is set, the program is in input mode.

$E02: SPCINIT   Special init byte used by some of the external modem drivers.

$E03: BYCNT   3-byte byte counting field. Bytes 0 and 1 are in the range 0-60 indicating seconds and minutes. Byte 2 is in the range 0-255 indicating hours connected. The modem driver computes how many bytes make up a second.

$E06: MDMINIT   Initialize the modem.

$E09: MDMRSET   Set up the modem to be able to receive an incoming call.

$E0C: MDMRING   Checks for a connection with a remote modem. If carry is set, a connection is established.

$E0F: MDMANS   Force the modem to answer the phone and attempt a connection.

$E12: MDMHANG   Hang up the modem.

$E15: MDMIN   Checks for and gets data from the modem. If data is not present, A will return zero and carry will be clear. If there is data, A will contain the data (without high-bit manipulation) and carry will be set.

$E18: MDMOUT   Send data to the modem. The data will be sent without high-bit manipulation. The byte counter is also updated by a MDMOUT call.

$E1B: MDMDCD   Checks the status of carrier with regard to the remote user. If carry returns set, a remote user is present. If carry returns clear, the remote user has hung up.

CHAPTER 7
Shell Listing

Logon Segment – LOGON.SEG.S

```
; ******************
; GBBS "Pro" V:2.2
; Copyright 1986-2023
; Kevin M. Smallwood
; ******************
; logon segment rev - 1/10/2023

    public get.pass
    clear
    set pa$=ram,8:set ph$=ram+8,12
    when$=ram+20:flag=ram+22
    nibble=ram+27:byte=ram+37
    sc$=chr$(12)

start
    modem(1):close
    open #1,"b:data"
    input #1,c1,c2,ct,ct$,da$
    input #1,nu,mn,wm,tm\lu$
    close:open #1,"b:data1"
    input #1,sn$\sys$\sv$
    input #1,md$\s$\n$
    input #1,lg,fv:close
    date$=da$:da$=date$:cn$=str$(c2)
    if ct$=da$ goto start1
    ct=1:ct$=da$:kill "b:log.daily"
    create "b:log.daily":open #1,"b:log.daily"
    print #1,"Name of user  Baud  Logoff time"\:close
start1
    if c1 cn$=str$(c1)+right$("000"+cn$,4)

    text:home
    print " ::::::::::::::::::::::::::::::::::::::::"
    print ': GBBS "Pro" V2.2                      :'
    print ': Copyright 1986-2023 Kevin Smallwood :'
    print ' ::::::::::::::::::::::::::::::::::::::::'

    print @(20-len(sn$)/2),6 sn$
```

```
      x$="Awaiting call "+cn$+" on "+da$
      print @(20-len(x$)/2),8 x$
      x$="This will be call "+str$(ct)+" today"
      print @(20-len(x$)/2),9 x$
; use "b:acos.time,20,20"
      modem(0):bb=0:home:clock(0)
      d=0:on nocar goto start
      tone(100,50):tone(125,50):tone(150,50):cm$=date$+" "+time$
      i$="":if info(0) goto online
      print "1) Auto Logon     2) Normal Logon"
      print "3) System Logon   4) Logon as a user"\
      print "Which ? ";:get i$
      if (i$="1") or (i$="Y") then x=1:i$="":goto autolog
      if (i$="3") or (i$="S") then x=1:i$="":d=19:goto autolog
      if (i$<>"4") and (i$<>"U") goto online
      input \"User number to log on as: " i$:x=val(i$):i$="":goto autolog

online
      print sc$:if info(0) print "Connect at ["info(2)*300"] baud!"\
      print \"(*> Welcome to "sn$" <*)"
      print \'New users type "NEW"'

logon
      print \"Account Number"
      un=0:input "-->" i$:x=val(i$)
      if i$="NEW" goto new.user
      print \"Enter Password"
      echo="X":input "-->" i$:echo=""
      print \"Verifying Account..."

logon2
      if (x<1) or (x>nu) goto bad.user
      i$=left$(i$+"        ",8)
autolog
      gosub rd.user:if d1$="" goto bad.user
      if i$=pa$ goto login
      if i$="" goto login

bad.user
      bb=bb+1
      if bb<3 print \"Incorrect, try again":goto logon
      print \"Illegal Access":goto start

; *** New User Logon ***

new.user
      print \"Enter your real full name [20 chars max]"
      input @3 ":" i$:if i$="" goto new.user
      if len(i$)>20 print \"20 characters only please.":goto new.user
      if instr(",",i$) print \"No commas please.":goto new.user
```

```
        d3$=i$:a$="":for l=1 to len(i$)
        x=asc(mid$(i$,l,1)):if x>96 then x=x-32
        a$=a$+chr$(x):next:x=instr(" ",a$)
        if not(x) d2$=a$:d1$=".":goto get.city
        d1$=left$(a$,x-1):d2$=mid$(a$,x+1)

get.city
        print \"City [16 chars max]"
        input ":" d4$
        if len(d4$)>16 print "Too long, try again":goto get.city

get.state
        print \"State [Form: XX]"
        input ":" d5$
        if len(d5$)<>2 print "Two letter code only.":goto get.state
        fill ram,58,0

get.phone
        print \"Phone number [Form: ###-###-####]"
        input ":" i$
        if len(i$)<>12 goto get.phone
        a$=left$(i$,3)+"-"+mid$(i$,5,3)+"-"+right$(i$,4)
        ph$=a$
        print \"We have the following."\
        print d3$\d4$", "d5$\ph$\:input @2 "Is this correct (Y/[N])? " i$
        if left$(i$,1)<>"Y" goto logon

get.guest
        nibble(0)=width(0)-1:edit(4)=0
        edit(3)=width(nibble(0)+1)-1
        nibble(5)=3:byte(7)=0
        print \'Type "P" for a password or "G" for'
        print "guest access."
        input @0 "-->" i$
        if i$="P" goto get.pass
        if i$<>"G" goto get.guest
        x=0:pa$="GUEST    ":flag(0)=1
        lc$="UNKNOWN":goto login

get.pass
        flag(0)=0:on nocar goto start
        print \"Finding your account."
        print \"Checking "nu" user files...[001]";
        open #1,"b:users"
        a=1:z=0:a$=d1$+","+d2$

add.user
        position #1,128,a
        input #1,b$,c$
        i$=b$+","+c$
```

```
     if a$=i$ close:print \\"Your name is being used.":goto logon

     if (i$=",") and (not z) then z=a
     a=a+1:if info(2)<>1 print chr$(8,4);right$("00"+str$(a),3)"]";
     if info(2)=1 if not (a mod 5) print chr$(8,4);right$("00"+str$
     (a),3)"]";
     if a<=nu goto add.user
     a=z:if not z then nu=nu+1:a=nu close
     print sc$:copy "sys.newinfo":x=0:print
     create "b:temp":open #1,"b:sys.questions":open #2,"b:temp"

info
     input #1,a$:if a$="*" goto info.1
     if eof(1) goto info.2
     print a$:goto info

info.1
     input \":" i$:print #2,i$:goto info

info.2
     print \"Would you like to leave the Sysop"
     input @2 "a Message (Y/[N]) ? " i$:if left$(i$,1)<>"Y" goto info.3
     print sc$"Enter message now, 40 colums, 4k max"
     print '".h" for help, "DONE" when finished'
     close #1:edit(0):edit(1):if not edit(2) goto info.3
     print #2:append #2:copy #8,#2:append #2:print #2

info.3
     close:edit(0):copy "b:temp",#8:kill "b:temp"
info.3a
     print \"Please enter a password [4-8 Characters]"
     input @2 ":" i$:if i$="" for x=1 to 5:i$=i$+rnd$:next
     x=len(i$):if x<4 print \"Password must be at least 4 chars":goto
     info.3a
     pa$=left$(i$+chr$(32,7),8)
     print \\"You will be user #"a
     print "Password will be :"pa$
     print \"Please write them down as you"
     print "will need them next time you call."
     when$=date$:open #1,"users"
     position #1,128,a
     print #1 d1$,d2$\d3$\d4$,d5$
     position #1,128,a,70
     write #1,ram,58:close

     create "b:request":open #1,"b:request":a$="(> "
     append #1:print #1,a\a$"NEW USER DATA"
     print #1,a$    ;d3$\a$;d4$", "d5$\a$;"#"a"-"pa$
     print #1,a$    ;ph$\a$;date$" "time$\:append #1
     copy #8,#1:append #1:print #1,chr$(1):close
```

```
      ready "g:mail":kill #msg(a):update
      print \"Press <CR> to enter "sn$;
      input @3 " " i$:x=a:i$=pa$:goto logon2

; *** Main Logon Routine ***

login
      if lc$<>date$ then nibble(6)=0:flag(36)=0:byte(7)=0
      lr=byte(5)+byte(6)*256:if lr>mn then lr=0
      nb=lr:un=x:info(3)=byte(0):b=byte(7):if flag(1) flag(0)=0
      if (b<nibble(5)*10) or flag(34) goto login1
      print \\"Daily time expired. Call tomorrow":goto start
login1
      if (flag(34) and (nibble(5)=0)) b=0:goto login1a
      b=((nibble(5)*10)-byte(7))*60
login1a
      clock(2)=b:b=((clock(2)-clock(1))/60)+1

; This code can be deleted if you are running a new 1.3 system
; or all users have logged on since the change over.

      if d4$="" gosub up.from

; the code above is for updating your 1.3 user file

      a1$=d1$:a2$=d2$:a3$=d3$:a4$=d4$:a5$=d5$
      tc=byte(1)+nibble(1)*256:bp=byte(2)+nibble(2)*256
      dl=byte(3)+nibble(3)*256:ul=byte(4)+nibble(4)*256
      info(5)=flag(34):if not flag(1) info(5)=0
      if (not info(5)) or (not info(0)) goto login2

      print \"Remote Password":echo="X":input "-->" i$
      echo="":if i$<>sv$ then info(5)=0

login2
      print sc$:gosub get.time
      print "Good "x$" "a3$","\"It's "time$" on "date$
      print "You were last on "lc$
      if not info(5) print "Time left today: "b" mins."\

      a$=right$("    "+str$(un),4):clear #9
      print #9,cn$,a1$" "a2$" of "a4$", "a5$,nibble(6)
      print #9,tc,ul,dl,bp,ph$,lc$,a$,pa$
      for x=1 to 34:print #9,flag(x);:next
      print ^

      if lr<wm then f$="b:sys.news":gosub show.file
      if lr+1=wm then lr=wm
      print \"Welcome to the board"
      print \"Sysop ->"sys$
```

```
     bb=1:ready "f:b1"
     print \"Main Bulletins from 1 to "msg(0)
     a=mn-lr:if lr=0 then a=tm
     if a print "There are "a" new bulletins"
     if not info(5) goto login3
     open #1,"b:request":a=mark(1):close
     if not a print "There are new users"
login3
     edit(4)=nibble(0)/4:ch=1:edit(3)=width((nibble(0) mod 4)+1)-1
     if (info(5)) and (d=19) link "a:system.seg"
     link "a:main.seg"

; *** Sub - Routines ***

rd.user
     open #1,"b:users"
     position #1,128,x
     input #1,d1$,d2$\d3$\d4$,d5$
     position #1,128,x,70
     read #1,ram,58
     lc$=mid$(" "+when$,2)
     close #1
     return

show.file
     setint(1):print \s$\:copy f$:setint(""):return

get.time
     x=val(left$(time$,2))
     if right$(time$,1)="M" goto get.t12
     if x<17 x$="afternoon":else x$="evening"
     if x<12 x$="morning"
     return
get.t12
; for 12 Hour Clocks
     x$="evening"
     if x<6 x$="afternoon"
     if right$(time$,2)="AM" x$="morning"
     return

; the code below is for update of the 1.2 user file
; delete if running new user file for 1.3.

up.from
     print \"City [16 chars max]"
     input ":" d4$
     if len(d4$)>16 print "Too long, try again":goto up.from

up.state
     print \"State [Form: XX]"
```

```
    input ":" d5$
    if len(d5$)<2 print "Two letter code please.":goto up.state
    if len(d5$)>2 print "Two letter code only.":goto up.state
    print \"We have the following."\
    print d4$", "d5$\:input @2 "Is this correct (Y/[N]) ? " i$
    if left$(i$,1)<>"Y" goto up.from
    return
```

Main Segment – MAIN.SEG.S

```
; ******************
; GBBS "Pro" V:2.2
; Copyright 1986-2023
;  Kevin M. Smallwood
; ******************
; main segment - 1/10/2023

    public fromsys
    public return
    public term1
    public termin2

    on nocar goto term1
    if flag(0) goto main
    if fv then a$="b:v1":gosub force
    ready "g:mail"
    if not msg(un) goto main
    print "You have mail waiting!"
    input @2 \"Read it now ([Y]/N) ?" i$
    if i$<>"N" then a$="rd.mail":gosub link.msg

fromsys
    on nocar goto term1

main
    x=(clock(2)-clock(1))/60:y=clock(2):x$=right$("0"+str$(x),2)
    if clock(1)>clock(2) x$="!!"
    if x=0 x$="--"
    if not y x$="**"
    if info(5) x$="::"
    print \"["x$"][Main Level] ";
    input "Option (?=Help):" i$:push main

main.cmd
    if i$="B" bb=1:a$="bulletins":goto link.msg
    if left$(i$,1)="B" a$="bulletins":goto bulletins
    if left$(i$,1)="J" a$="bulletins":goto bulletins
```

```
     if i$="R" then a$="rd.mail":goto link.msg
     if (i$="?" or i$="/") goto menu
     if i$="C" goto chat
     if i$="D" goto display
     if i$="F" goto feedback
     if i$="T" goto terminate
     if i$="E" goto show.stat
     if i$="$" f$="b:sys.news":goto show.file
     if i$="H" f$="b:hlp.main":goto show.file
     if i$="I" f$="b:sys.info":goto show.file
     if (i$="P") and (flag(0)) goto getpass
     if (i$="%") and (info(5)) pop:link "a:system.seg"
     if not(flag(1) or info(5)) goto main2

     if i$="S" a$="sd.mail":goto link.msg
     if i$="P" goto setpass
     if i$="U" goto userlist
     if i$="V" a$="b:v1":goto voting
     if i$="G" a$="c:g1":goto general
     if i$="Q" bb=1:a$="bulletins":goto link.msg
     if i$="O" f$="b:bbs":goto show.file
     if i$="L" f$="b:log.daily":goto show.file
     if i$="X" a$="d:d1":goto download

main2
     a1=a1+1:print \'Sorry, "'i$'" is not a command.':if a1<3 return

; *** sub - routines ***
; On the fly menus

menu
     a1=0:f$="b:mnu.new"
     if not (flag(1)) goto menu.1
     if (edit(3)<79) f$="b:mnu.val.40":else f$="b:mnu.val.80"
menu.1
     open #1,f$:input #1,x$:setint(" "):for l=1 to len(x$)
     addint(mid$(x$,l,1)):next:print \sc$\
     copy #1:if key(3) goto menu.key
     a=key(0):close:setint(""):pop:goto main

menu.key
     close:setint(""):a=key(0)
     if (a>96) and (a<123) a=a-32
     if a=32 pop:goto main
     print:i$=chr$(a):print i$:goto main.cmd

; terminate from system and recycle

terminate
     print \"Terminate Connection"
```

```
      input @2 \"Are you sure (Y/[N]) ?" i$
      if left$(i$,1)<>"Y" return
termin2
      on nocar goto term5
      if (not ma) or (not flag(34)) goto term1
      if ma and flag(34) input @2 \"Delete Mail ([Y]/N) ?" i$:if i$=""
      i$="Y"
      i$=left$(i$,1):ma=(i$="Y")
term1
      on nocar clear
      print \"Goodbye "a3$","\"you were caller #"cn$
      print \"Thank you for calling "sn$:a=clock(1)
      if a print \"Connected "a/60" mins, "a mod 60" secs"
      print \md$\"       GBBS Pro V:2.2n" \"   (C)1986-2023 Kevin
      Smallwood" \md$
      close:log "b:":modem(1):if a1$="" goto term4
      if not un goto term3
term2
      open #1,"b:users":nibble(6)=nibble(6)+1:tc=tc+1
      byte(1)=tc mod 256:nibble(1)=tc/256
      byte(2)=bp mod 256:nibble(2)=bp/256
      byte(3)=dl mod 256:nibble(3)=dl/256
      byte(4)=ul mod 256:nibble(4)=ul/256
      byte(5)=lr mod 256:byte(6)=lr/256
      byte(0)=info(3):when$="x"

; to enable the time per day mod remove the ';' from the line below
; byte(7)=(byte(7)+(clock(1)/60))

      position #1,128,un
      print #1,a1$,a2$\a3$\a4$,a5$
      position #1,128,un,70
      write #1,ram,58:close
term3
      if not info(5) then ct=ct+1:c2=c2+1
      if c2>9999 then c2=0:c1=c1+1
      open #1,"data":print #1,c1,c2,ct,ct$,date$
      print #1,nu,mn,wm,tm\a1$" "a2$:close
      if ma ready "g:mail":kill #msg(un):update
      if (lg=0) or (info(5)) goto term4
      create "b:log.system":open #1,"b:log.system":append #1
      print #1,"Call #"cn$" / Connected at "cm$" / "a3$" of "a4$",
      "a5$
      print #1,"Last date on "lc$" / "ph$" / "un"-"pa$;
      print #1," / Speed = "info(2)*300" baud"
      for x=1 to 8:print #1,flag(x);:next:a=clock(1)
      print #1," / Connected "a/60" mins, "a mod 60" secs"\:close
      open #1,"b:log.daily":append #1
      print #1,left$(a3$+"...................",20);
      z$="  0000":z$=left$(z$,6-(len(str$(info(2)*300))))+str$(in
```

```
      fo(2)*3 00)
      print #1,z$" "time$:close
term4
      link "a:logon.seg"
term5
      ma=0:goto term1

; chat with sysop

chat
      if ch>6 print \"You were warned.  Goodbye!":goto term1
      if ch>5 print \"Once more and you`ll be logged off":ch=ch+1
      if ch>3 print \"Sysop is not available":ch=ch+1:return
      print \"Paging Sysop: ";:tone(100,100,100)
      if flag(2) tone (125,100,100):tone(150,100,100)
      print "Continue...":info(4)=1:ch=ch+1:return

; show user's status

show.stat
      print \"    Your Status"\
      print "Name -> "a3$
      print "From -> "a4$", "a5$
      print "Phone # "ph$
      print "User  # "un
      print "Last On : "lc$
      print "Level # : ";
      for x=1 to 8:print flag(x);:next
      print \\"Last Caller: "lu$
      print \"You are caller : "cn$
      print "Todays  calls : "ct\
      print "Logon time : "cm$
      print "Actual time: "date$" "time$:a=clock(1)
      print "Connected   : "a/60" mins, "a mod 60" secs"
      b=clock(2):if b print "Time left   : "(b-a)/60" mins"
      print \"[ Options Available ]"\
      open #1,"b:data2":z=0:for x=0 to 34:a$=""
      if flag(x) position #1,32,x:input #1,a$
      if a$<>"" setint(1):print a$:z=1:if key(1) then x=34
      next:close:if not z print "Limited system access"
      setint(""):return

; show list of system users

userlist
      print \"List of System Users"\
      input @2 "Match letters (<CR>=All,?):" i$
      if i$="?" f$="b:hlp.user":gosub show.file:goto userlist
      m$="":if info(5) input @0 \"Show passwords ?" m$
      print \s$:open #1,"b:users":x=1
```

```
     if left$(i$,1)="#" x=val(mid$(i$,2)):i$=""
     if (x=0) or (x>nu) then x=1
usrlst2
     position #1,128,x:input #1,a$,b$
     if a$="" goto usrlst3
     a$=a$+" "+b$:setint(1)
     if not instr(i$,a$) goto usrlst3
     input #1,c$\d$,e$:position #1,128,x,70
     move ram,58 to ram2:on nocar goto usrlst4:read #1,ram,58
     setint(1):print \"#"x" "c$" ][ On: "when$\"From: "d$", "e$;
     if (m$<>"") or (mid$(ph$,4,1)=" ") print " ][ "ph$:else print
     if m$="Y" print "Pass: "pa$" ][ Time: "nibble(5)*10
     move ram2,58 to ram:on nocar goto term1
usrlst3
     if (not key(1)) and (x<nu) then x=x+1:goto usrlst2
     setint(""):close:return
usrlst4
     move ram2,58 to ram:goto term1

; file transfer section

download
     open #1,a$:input #1,x,d3$:close
     if d3$<>"" d3$=chr$(13)+d3$+chr$(13)
     b$=left$(a$,instr(":",a$))
down2
     print d3$\"Download Files 1-"x" [L]ist Files"
     input "[U]pload a File [H]elp [Q]uit ?" i$
     a=val(i$):if i$="Q" return
     if i$="U" goto upload
     if i$="L" goto down3
     if i$="H" then f$="b:help.xfer":gosub show.file:goto down2
     if (a=0) or (a>x) goto down2
     print \"A)scii, D)os Xmodem, P)roDOS Xmodem"
     input @0 "S)tandard Xmodem (ibm,trs), Q)uit ?" i$
     z=9:if i$="S" then z=0
     if i$="P" then z=1
     if i$="D" then z=2
     if i$="A" then z=3
     if z=9 goto down2
     open #1,a$:input #1,x:y=0
down2a
     if eof(1) close:goto down2
     input #1,i$:if left$(i$,1)<>">" goto down2a
     y=y+1:if a<>y goto down2a:else y=instr("^",i$)
     if y f$=b$+mid$(i$,y+1):else f$=b$+mid$(i$,3)
     close:open #1,f$:if mark(1) close:goto down2
     i$=mid$(i$,3):if y i$=left$(i$,y-4)
     print \"Sending "i$", "size(1)*2+1" blocks":close
     input @3 \"Press <CR> to begin" i$
```

```
     byte(2)=byte(2)+1:use "b:x.dn",z,f$:goto down2
down3
     print:open #1,a$:input #1,x:a=1
     if not x close:print \"No downloads today":goto down2
down4
     input #1,i$:z=instr("^",i$):if z=0 z=len(i$)+1
     if left$(i$,1)=")" print a;:a=a+1:i$=left$(i$,z-1)
     setint(1):print i$:if not(eof(1) or key(1)) goto down4
     close:setint(""):goto down2

upload
     if not flag(2) print \"Security too low":goto down2
     print \"Upload a file"\\"A)scii, D)os Xmodem, P)roDOS Xmodem"
     input @0 "S)tandard Xmodem (ibm,trs), Q)uit ?" i$
     z=9:if i$="S" then z=0
     if i$="P" then z=1
     if i$="D" then z=2
     if i$="A" then z=3
     if z=9 goto down2
     y=1:f$=""
upload2
     input @2 \"Filename:" f$:if f$="" goto upload
     if not info(5) then f$="e:u"+str$(un)+"."+f$
     if not instr(":",f$) then f$="e:"+f$
     if len(f$)>17 print \"Illegal filename":goto upload2
     open #1,f$:a=mark(1):close:if a goto upload3
     if info(5)=0 print \"Filename in use":goto upload2
     input @0 \"Filename in use: Overwrite ?" i$
     if i$<>"Y" goto upload2
upload3
     create f$:open #1,f$:a=mark(1):close
     if a print \"Illegal filename":goto upload2
     if z<>3 input @3 \"Press <CR> to begin" i$
     nibble(3)=nibble(3)+1
     use "b:x.up",z,f$:goto down2

; feedback to sysop

feedback
     print \"Feedback to Sysop"
     input @3 \"Subject:" sb$:if sb$="" sb$="None"
     gosub editor:if not edit(2) return
     h$="      --> Feedback from a User <--"
     d=1:print \"Wait...";:a$="wr.letter"
     gosub link.msg:print ".Feedback saved":return

; general files

general
     open #1,a$:input #1,x
```

```
      if not x close:print \"No Active Files":return
      print \s$\:setint(1):gosub showfl2
general2
      print \"Which 1-"x" (?=Menu,<CR>):";
      input @3 i$:if i$="" return
      if i$="?" goto general
      a=val(i$):if (not a) or (a>x) goto general2
      f$=a$+"."+str$(a):gosub show.file:goto general2


; set display characteristics

display
      print \"Display Characteristics"\
      print "Video width now = "edit(3)+1
      print "Back-space mode = ";
      a=nibble(0)/4:if a=1 print "non-";
      if a=0 print "Unknown":else print "destruct"
      print "Nulls sent @ LF = "info(3)
      print "Page pause mode = ";
      if flag(35) print "ON":else print "OFF"
      print "Show phone numb = ";
      if mid$(ph$,4,1)=" " print "YES":else print "NO"
display2
      input @0 \"Set: [V, B, N, P, S, or Q=Quit] ?" i$
      if i$="Q" return
      if i$="B" goto backspace
      if i$="S" goto phone
      if i$="N" goto nulls
      if i$="P" goto paging
      if i$<>"V" goto display2

video
      print \"Set Video Width"
      print \"New width (";
      print width(1),width(2),width(3),width(4);
      input @2 ") ?" i$:if i$="" goto display2
      a=val(i$):for x=1 to 4
      if a=width(x) nibble(0)=nibble(0)/4*4+(x-1):edit(3)=a-1
      next:print \"Video width = "edit(3)+1:goto display

backspace
      print \"Set Cursor Characteristics"
      print \"123456" chr$(8,3):a=0
      print \"How many numbers do you see"\
      print "3 shows a destructable backspace"
      print "6 shows a non-destructable backspace"
      input @2 \"How many (3 or 6) ?" i$
      if i$="" goto display2
      if i$="6" then a=1
```

```
      if i$="3" then a=2
      nibble(0)=(nibble(0) mod 4)+(a*4)
      edit(4)=a:goto display

nulls
      print \"Set new null value"
      input @2 \"Set to (0-127):" i$
      if i$<>"" then info(3)=val(i$)
      goto display

phone
      ph$=left$(ph$,3)+"-"+mid$(ph$,5)
      input @2 \"Show phone number to other users ?" i$
      i$=left$(i$,1):if i$<>"Y" goto display
      ph$=left$(ph$,3)+" "+mid$(ph$,5):goto display

paging
      print \"Pause after page"
      input @2 \"Set paging (ON,OFF):" i$
      if i$="ON" flag(35)=1
      if i$="OFF" flag(35)=0
      goto display

; get a password for guests

getpass
      print \"Do you wish to receive a password to"
      input @0 "log in with the next time you call ?" i$
      if i$<>"Y" return
      d1$=a1$:d2$=a2$:d3$=a3$
      link "a:logon.seg","get.pass"

; get a new password

setpass
      print \"Change your Password"
      input @2 \"Enter your current password: "; i$
      if i$="" return
      i$=left$(i$+"    ",8):if i$<>pa$ print \"Incorrect!":return
      print \"Your password may be 4-8 chars long"
      echo="X":input @2 \"Enter your new password: "; i$
      if i$="" then echo="":return
      input @2 "Please type it in again: " a$
      echo="":a=len(i$)
      if a$<>i$ print \"Passwords do not match":return
      if (a<4) or (a>8) print \"Password must be 4-8 chars":return
      pa$=left$(i$+"    ",8):print \"New Password Accepted":return

; do voting section
```

```
force
    if not flag(1) then return
    open #1,a$:mark(1)=(un/512)*64:fill ram2,64,0
    read #1,ram2,64:z=flag:flag=ram2:a=flag(un)
    flag=z:close:if a return

voting
    setint(""):create a$:open #1,a$
    mark(1)=(un/512)*64:x=mark(1):fill ram2,64,0
    read #1,ram2,64:z=flag:flag=ram2:a=flag(un)
    flag(un)=1:flag=z:mark(1)=x:write #1,ram2,64
    x=1:z=byte:byte=ram2
vote2
    open #2,a$+"."+str$(x):if mark(2) goto vote5
    input #2,y:if a then setint(1)
    print \s$\:copy #2:position #1,32,x+7
    fill ram2,32,0:read #1,ram2,32
    b=byte(0)+byte(1)*256:if a goto vote4
vote3
    print \"Vote (1-"y",S=Skip):";
    input i$:if i$="S" goto vote4
    d=val(i$):if (d<1) or (d>y) goto vote3
    b=b+1:byte(0)=b mod 256:byte(1)=b/256
    c=byte(d*2)+byte(d*2+1)*256:c=c+1
    byte(d*2)=c mod 256:byte(d*2+1)=c/256
    position #1,32,x+7:write #1,ram2,32
vote4
    if key(1) then close:return
    print \"Results from "b" users:"\:b=b+(b=0)
    for c=1 to y:y=byte(c*2)+byte(c*2+1)*256
    print "Answer "c" - "(y*100)/b"%"
    next:close #2:x=x+1:goto vote2
vote5
    close:byte=z:return

; bulletins / e-mail

bulletins
    if len(i$)<2 goto link.msg
    a=val(mid$(i$,2)):if a then bb=a
link.msg
    link "a:msg.seg",a$
return
    on nocar goto term1
    return

; *** sub - routines ***

; enter a message
```

```
editor
     on nocar goto editor1
     print \"Enter message now, "edit(3)" cols, [4k] max"
     print '[DONE] when finished, [.H] for help'
     cl=clock(2):clock(2)=0:edit(0):edit(1):clock(2)=cl
     on nocar goto term1:return
editor1
     pop:clock(2)=cl:goto term1


; show a disk file

show.file
     setint(1):print \s$\:open #1,f$:if mark(1) close #1:return
showfl2
     copy (20) #1
     if (eof(1) or key(1)) setint(""):close #1:return
     if not flag(35) goto showfl2
     print "Press [RETURN] ";:get i$:if i$=chr$(13) print " ";
     print chr$(8,16);chr$(32,16);chr$(8,16);
     if i$=" " setint(""):close #1:return
     setint(1):goto showfl2
```

Message Segment – MSG.SEG.S

```
; ******************
; GBBS "Pro" V:2.2
; Copyright 1986-2023
;   Kevin M. Smallwood
; ******************
; msg segment - 1/10/2023

     public bulletins
     public rd.mail
     public sd.mail
     public wr.letter

bulletins
     zz=0:fl=peek(2053)*256:pf=peek(fl):gosub start
     flag(37)=1:gosub pfilter:goto link.main
rd.mail
     gosub rd.mail0:goto link.main
sd.mail
     gosub snd.mail:goto link.main
wr.letter
     s=8:gosub wr.ltr
```

```
link.main
    link "a:main.seg","return"
link.term
    link "a:main.seg","termin2"

; *** bulletins / e-mail ***

start
    on nocar goto link.term
    gosub idinf
    if bf$="" print \"That board is down right now.":gosub cmd2c:return
    if not b1 print \"You do not have access to that board.":gosub
    cmd2c:return
    if i$="Q" gosub qscan
cmd1
    if msg(0) goto cmd2
    print \"The "bn$\" has no bulletins...";
    input @2 "Post a bulletin ([Y]/N) ?" i$
    if left$(i$,1)="N" return
    sb$="":ti$="All":d=0:gosub post:if not b2 return
    goto cmd1

cmd2
    x=(clock(2)-clock(1))/60:y=clock(2):x$=right$("0"+str$(x),2)
    if clock(1)>clock(2) x$="!!"
    if x=0 x$="--"
    if not y x$="**"
    if info(5) x$="::"
    free:print \bn$\"["x$"][Board #"bb"  1-"msg(0)"] ";
    input "Option (?=Help):" i$
cmd2a
    zz=0:a=val(i$):push cmd2
    if left$(i$,1)="J" then i$=mid$(i$,2):goto jmp3
    if left$(i$,1)="F" goto fwd
    if left$(i$,1)="R" goto rvs
    if left$(i$,1)="K" goto kill
    if left$(i$,1)="S" goto scan
    if i$="A" or i$="Q" pop:return
    if i$="M" goto mark
    if i$="N" goto new
    if i$="B" goto browse
    if i$="G" goto qscan
    if i$="H" f$="b:hlp.msg":goto show.file
    if i$="J" y=0:goto jump
    if i$="P" then ti$="All":sb$-"":d=0:goto post
    if i$="L" y=1:goto list
    if i$="T" goto terminate
    if i$=">" and (bb<ab) bb=bb+1:zz=1:pop:goto start
    if i$="<" and (bb>1) bb=bb-1:zz=2:pop:goto start
    if (a>0) and (a<=msg(0)) i$="F"+i$:goto fwd
```

```
    if i$="?" or i$="/" goto cmd.menu
    a1=a1+1:print \'Sorry, "'i$'" is not a command. (?=Help)':if a1<3
    return

cmd.menu
    a1=0:print \bn$\'
    Read #, OR: [N]ew   [F#]orward [S#]can [B]rowse [M]arked [L]ist
        [R#]vse [G]lobal   [J#]ump [P]ost   [K#]ill  [H]elp
        [Q]uit  [>] Next board      [<] Previous board

    Command letters followed with "#" have a numeric argument option.
    "F45" reads F)orward beginning at bulletin 45
    "K32" would K)ill bulletin #32"
':return

cmd2c
    if not zz return
    if zz=1 bb=bb+1
    if zz=2 bb=bb-1
    zz=0:pop:goto start

; terminate connection

terminate
    print \"Terminate Connection"
    input @2 \"Are you sure (Y/[N]) ?" i$
    if left$(i$,1)<>"Y" return
    link "a:main.seg","termin2"

; post a bulletin

post
    if not b2 print \"You do not have access to that board.":return
    edit(0):if kl goto post2
    if msg(0)=mb print \"Sorry, no room on this board.":return
    if msg(0)=info(1) print \"Board directory full.":return
    if info(6)<29 print \"Board bit-map full.":return
post2
    print \"Post Bulletin"\
    if d open #1,"b:users":position #1,128,d:input #1,d1$,d2$\d3$:close
    if d ti$=d3$+" (#"+str$(d)+")":if d=1 ti$="Sysop"
    if ti$<>"" print "  To ->"ti$" ([Y]/N):";: get i$
    if i$=chr$(13) n=9:gosub backup:print:goto post2a
    if i$="N" n=len(ti$)+10:gosub backup:input @4 ti$:if ti$="" return
    if (ti$<>"") and left$(i$,1)<>"N" n=10:gosub backup:print
    if ti$="" input @4 "  To ->"ti$:if ti$="" return
post2a
    i$="":if sb$<>"" print " Sub ->"sb$" ([Y]/N):";:get i$
    if i$=chr$(13) n=9:gosub backup:print:goto post2b
    if i$="N" n=len(sb$)+10:gosub backup:input @4 a$:if a$="" return
```

```
      if (sb$<>"" or a$<>"") and left$(i$,1)<>"N" n=10:gosub
      backup:print
      if sb$="" input @4 " Sub ->"a$:if a$="" return
      if a$<>"" sb$=a$
post2b
      a$=a3$:if (un=bs) and  (bs$<>"") a$=bs$
      a$=a$+" (#"+str$(un)+")"
      if not info(5) goto post2c
      i$="":print "From ->"a$" ([Y]/N):";:get i$
      if i$=chr$(13) n=9:gosub backup:print:goto post2c
      if i$="N" n=len(a$)+10:gosub backup:input @3 a$:if a$="" return
      if (a$<>"") and left$(i$,1)<>"N" n=10:gosub backup:print
post2c
      i$="":if flag(36) print \"Anonymous Posting (Y/[N]):";:get
      i$:print
      if (flag(36)) and (i$="Y") flag(38)=1:else flag(38)=0
      input @2 \"Post: [Y]es, N)o, X)modem " i$
      if i$="N" return
      if i$="X" gosub up.xmdm:else gosub editor
      if not edit(2) return
      print \edit(2)" bytes entered"
      print "Saving Message...wait..";:bp=bp+1
      if (kl>0) and (kl<=msg(0)) kill #msg(kb):crunch:b=b-1
      a=msg(0)+1
      if flag(38) print #msg(a),"*"sb$:else print #msg(a),sb$
      print #6,tn,ti$
      if flag(38) print #6,0,a$:else print #6,un,a$
      if flag(38) print #6,"Date ->"date$\:else print #6,"Date
      ->"date$"  "time$\
      copy #8,#6:msg(a)=mn:mn=mn+1:update:tm=tm+1
      print ".saved":ti$="":a$="":return

; show new bulletins

new
      print \"New Bulletins"
      if nn>msg(msg(0)) print \"No new bulletins":return
      x=msg(0):if not lr a=1:goto fwd2
new1
      if nn=<msg(x) a=x:x=x-1:if x goto new1
      goto fwd2

; bulletin retrieval - Forward

fwd
      if len(i$)>1 a=val(mid$(i$,2)):goto fwd1
      print \"Sequential Retrieval - Forward"
      input @2 \"Start where (#, F)irst, <CR>):" i$
      a=val(i$):if i$="F" a=1
fwd1
```

```
        if a<1 return
        if a>msg(0) a=msg(0)
fwd2
        print \s$\n$
fwd3
        gosub show:if x return
        if a<msg(0) then a=a+1:goto fwd3
        return



; bulletin retrieval - Reverse

rvs
        if len(i$)>1 a=val(mid$(i$,2)):goto rvs1
        print \"Sequential Retrieval - Reverse"
        input @2 \"Start where (#, L)ast, <CR>):" i$
        a=val(i$):if i$="L" a=msg(0)
rvs1
        if a<1 return
        if a>msg(0) a=msg(0)
rvs2
        print \s$\n$
rvs3
        gosub show:if x return
        if a>1 then a=a-1:goto rvs3
        return

; kill bulletins

kill
        if len(i$)>1 a=val(mid$(i$,2)):goto kill.1
        print \"Kill a Bulletin"
        input @2 \"Kill Bulletin (#,<CR>):" a
kill.1
        if (a<1) or (un=0) return
        if a>msg(0) print \"That Bulletin Does Not Exist!":return
        input #msg(a),a$\x,b$\x,c$
        if (info(5)) or (un=bs) goto kill.2
        if x<>un print \"Thats not your bulletin!":return
kill.2
        if (flag(38)) and (left$(a$,1)="*") a$=mid$(a$,2)
        print \"Numb ->"a" of "msg(0)\" Sub ->"a$
        input @2 \"Kill this bulletin (Y/[N]) ?" i$
        if left$(i$,1)<>"Y" return
kill.3
        tm=tm-1:y=msg(msg(0)):kill #msg(a):crunch
        b=msg(0):if b then msg(b)=y:update
        print \"Bulletin #"a" killed..."
        return
```

```
; browse bulletins titles

browse
     m$="":a=0:print \"Scan Bulletin Titles"
     print \"Scan for what text [<CR>=Everything]?"
     input @3 ":" m$:a=1:if m$="" a=0:return
     goto scan.2




; scan bulletins

scan
     print \"Scan bulletins"
     if len(i$)>1 a=val(mid$(i$,2):goto scan.1
     input @3 \"Start at (#,<CR>):"a
scan.1
     m$="":if a<1 return
     if a>msg(0) print \"That Bulletin Does Not Exist!":return
scan.2
     input @2 \"Allow marking (Y/[N]) ?" i$
     ms=0:if left$(i$,1)="Y" ms=a
     d=0:x=15:print:z=flag:flag=ram2
scan.3
     a$=" ":if msg(a)>nn then a$="*"
     flag(a-ms)=0:input #msg(a),t$\b,b$
     if m$ if not instr(m$,t$) goto scan.4
     if left$(t$,1)="*" t$=mid$(t$,2)
     x=x-1:d=d+1:print a$a". "t$\"   Addressed to:"b$\
     if i$<>"Y" goto scan.4
     print "Mark (Y/[N]/Q) ?";:get a$:print
     if a$="Q" goto scan.5
     flag(a-ms)=(a$="Y")
scan.4
     if a=msg(0) goto scan.5
     a=a+1:if x goto scan.3
     input @2 \"More ([Y]/N/C) ?" a$
     if left$(a$,1)="C" x=msg(0)-a-1:goto scan.3
     if left$(a$,1)<>"N" print:x=15:goto scan.3
scan.5
     me=a:flag=z:if not (d) print "Sorry, no match":ms=0:return
     if left$(i$,1)<>"Y" return

; marked bulletins retrieval

mark
     print \"Retrieve marked bulletins":a=ms
     if not ms print \"No marked bulletins":return
mark.2
```

```
    z=flag:flag=ram2:b=flag(a-ms):flag=z
    x=0:if b gosub show
    if x=0 a=a+1:if a<me goto mark.2
    return

; jump to another board.

jump
    print \"Jump to Another Board"
jmp2
    print \"Jump to (1-"ab",?,<CR>):";
    input @2 i$:if i$="" return
jmp3
    a=val(i$)
    if (a>0) and (a<=ab) pop:bb=a:goto start
    if i$<>"?" goto jmp2

; list of available boards.

list
    print sc$\s$\:open #1,"b:data2"
    for x=1 to ab:position #1,128,x+8
    input #1,a$\b$\a:setint(1)
    if instr(left$(a$,1),"#$%") a$=mid$(a$,2)
    b=1:if a then b=flag(a)
    if b and (b$<>"") print x". "a$
    if key(1) setint(""):x=ab
    next:close:if y return:else goto jmp2

; global quickscan

qscan
    ob=bb:bb=1
    print \"Global Quickscan...Spacebar Exits"
qs1
    setint (1):print \"Checking board: [";
qs2
    i$="":a$=right$("0"+str$(bb),2)
    print a$"]"      ;:gosub idinf:setint(1):if key(1) goto qs4
    if (not b1) or (bf$="") or (msg(0)=0) goto qs3
    if nn>msg(msg(0)) goto qs3
    print \\"The "bn$\"contains new message(s)"
    input @2 \"[R]ead S)kip Q)uit ?" i$
    if left$(i$,1)="Q" return
    if left$(i$,1)="S" goto qs3
    gosub new:input @2 \"Post a message (Y/[N]) ? " i$
    if i$="Y" sb$="":ti$="":gosub post
    i$="Y"
qs3
    bb=bb+1:if bb>ab goto qs4
```

```
     if i$<>"" goto qs1
     print chr$(8,3);:goto qs2
qs4
     if i$="" or i$=" " print
     setint(""):bb=ob:goto idinf

; bulletin show routine

show
     if nn<=msg(a) then nn=msg(a)+1
     x=0:if lr<=msg(a) then lr=msg(a)+1
show1
     if flag(36) goto anony
     input #msg(a),sb$\tn,ti$\d,fr$:setint(2)
     print #x,\" Brd ->"bn$\"Numb ->"a" of "msg(0)\" Sub ->"sb$
     print #x," To ->"ti$
     print #x,"From ->"fr$
show1a
     copy #6,#x:x=0:setint("")
     if key(1) x=1:return
     if key(2) return
show2
     if i$="+" return
     print \"[B"bb" #"a" of "msg(0)"] ? or Cmd [N]#";
     get i$:print
     if i$="?" print \"M)ail [N]ext R)eread X)modem Q)uit D)ump ";
     if i$="?" and (d=un or info(5)) print "E)dit K)ill ";
     if i$="?" and info(5) print "S)wap P)rint"
     if i$="?" print
     if i$="D" i$="+":return
     if i$="N" or i$=chr$(13) or i$="+" return
     if i$="Q" x=1:return
     if i$="R" goto show
     if i$="P" and info(5) x=5:goto show1
     if (i$="A" or i$="M") and flag(1) a$="":goto show5
     if i$="A" or i$="M" print \"Security too low":goto show2
     if i$="X" goto dn.xmdm
     if not flag(1) goto show2
     if not((d=un) or (info(5))) goto show2
     if i$="E" and (flag(2) or info(5)) goto show4
     if i$="W" and info(5) goto wrt.msg
     if i$="S" and info(5) goto mov.msg
     if i$<>"K" goto show2
     input @2 \"Kill: Are you Sure (Y/[N]) ?" i$
     if left$(i$,1)<>"Y" goto show2
     gosub kill.3:a=a-1:return
show4
     input @2 \"Edit: Are you Sure (Y/[N]) ?" i$
     if left$(i$,1)<>"Y" goto show2
     edit(0):input #msg(a),a$\b,b$\c,c$\d$\e$
```

```
     copy #6,#8:edit(1):if not edit(2) goto show2
     x=msg(a):kill #msg(a):print #msg(a),a$\b,b$\c,c$\d$\e$
     copy #8,#6:msg(a)=x:update:goto show2
show5
     input @2 \"Is this a private letter (Y/[N]) ?" i$
     if left$(i$,1)="Y" goto show6
     if (d=0 and flag(36)) ti$="Anoymous User":goto show5a
     open #1,"b:users":position #1,128,d
     input #1,d1$,d2$\d3$:close:ti$=d3$
show5a
     if left$(sb$,3)<>"Re:" then sb$="Re: "+sb$
     b=a:gosub post:a=b:goto show2
show6
     if d=0 print \"Sorry, anonymous sender":goto show2
     gosub editor:if not edit(2) goto show2
     print \edit(2)" bytes entered"
     print "Wait.." ;:s=8:gosub wr.ltr
     ready bf$:print ".reply sent":goto show2

wrt.msg
     input @2 \"Filename (to write):" i$
     if i$="" goto show2
     create i$:open #1,i$:append #1
     copy #msg(a),#1:close:goto show2


mov.msg
; Bulletin Mover From Al Anderson
     print \\"Bulletin Mover Utility"\\"Boards 1-"ab
     input @2 \"Move this post to board #" i$:zx=val(i$)
     if (zx>ab) or (zx<1) goto show2
     edit(0):input #msg(a),a$\b,b$\c,c$:copy #6,#8
     x=msg(a):b5=bb:bb=zx:gosub idinf
     if (kl>0)and(kl<=msg(0)) kill #msg(kb):crunch
     zx=msg(0)+1:print #msg(zx),a$\b,b$\c,c$:copy
     #8,#6:msg(a)=zx:update
     bb=b5:gosub idinf:msg(a)=x:print "On this board...";:gosub
     kill.3:a=a-1
     print "Bulletin is now on other board.":goto show2

;show a bulletin on anonymous boards.

anony
     input #msg(a),sb$\tn,ti$\d,fr$:setint(2)
     if left$(sb$,1)="*" sb$=mid$(sb$,2):goto anony1
     print #x,\" Brd ->"bn$\"Numb ->"a" of "msg(0)\" Sub ->"sb$
     print #x," To ->"ti$
     print #x,"From ->"fr$
     goto show1a
anony1
     print #x,\" Brd ->"bn$\"Numb ->"a" of "msg(0)\" Sub ->"sb$
```

```
      print #x,"  To ->"ti$
      if info(5) print #x,"From ->"fr$:goto show1a
      print #x,"From ->Anonymous Poster":goto show1a

;xmodem d/l of bulletin by Keith Christian

dn.xmdm
      print \"Download bulletin #"a;
      input @2 " via Xmodem (Y/[N]) ?" i$
      if left$(i$,1)<>"Y" return
      f$="b:d":create f$:ready bf$:open #1,f$
      input #msg(a),sb$\b,ti$\c,fr$:setint(2)
      y=0:if left$(sb$,1)="*" sb$=mid$(sb$,2):y=1
      print #1,\" Brd ->"bn$\"Numb ->"a" of "msg(0)\" Sub ->"sb$
      print #1,"  To ->"ti$
      if y print #1,"From ->Anonymous Poster":else print #1,"From
      ->"fr$
      copy #6,#1:close:print \"Ready to Send..."
      use "b:protocol.down",300,0,f$:kill f$:goto show2

;xmodem u/l of bulletin by Keith Christian

up.xmdm
      input @2 \"Upload a message via Xmodem ([Y]/N) ?" i$
      if i$="N" pop:return
      print \"Ready to Receive..."
      f$="b:u":use "b:protocol.up",300,0,f$
      close:edit(0):copy f$,#8
      print \edit(2)" bytes received"
      kill f$:edit(1):return

idinf
      flag(36)=0:flag(37)=1:flag(38)=0
      if bb=0 then bf$="":bl=0:return
      me=0:bl=bb:open #1,"b:data2"
      mark(1)=1120:input #1,ab
      if bb>ab close:bf$="":bl=0:return
      position #1,128,bb+8
      input #1,bn$\bf$\b3,b4\bs,bs$\mb,kl,kb
      if left$(bn$,1)="%" flag(36)=1:flag(37)=1:bn$=mid$(bn$,2)
      if left$(bn$,1)="$" flag(36)=1:flag(37)=0:bn$=mid$(bn$,2)
      if left$(bn$,1)="#" flag(36)=0:flag(37)=0:bn$=mid$(bn$,2)
      b1=1:if b3 then b1=flag(b3)
      b2=1:if b4 then b2=flag(b4)
      close:if bf$="" then bl=0:return
      if (b1) ready bf$:nn=nb
pfilter
      if not flag(37) poke fl,0:else poke fl,pf
      return
```

```
; read e-mail

rd.mail0
    on nocar goto link.term
    print \"Read Mail"
    if flag(0) print \"Guests can not receive mail":return
    ready "g:mail"
    if not msg(un) print \"No mail for you":return
    ready #msg(un)
rd.mail2
    x=0:input #7,i$:d=val(i$)
    if i$="" then ma=1:return
rd.mail3
    print #x,\md$:setint (2):copy #7,#x
    setint (""):print #x,md$
    if key(2) goto rd.mail2
rd.mail4
    input @2 \"(A)uto reply, [C]ontinue, (R)e-read :" i$
    if i$="" or i$="C" or i$="N" goto rd.mail2
    if i$="Q" return
    if i$="R" rewind:x=0:goto rd.mail3
    if i$="P" and info(5) rewind:x=5:goto rd.mail3
    if i$="W" and info(5) goto wr.mail
    if i$="F" goto forward
    if i$<>"A" goto rd.mail4
    if d=0 print \"Sorry, anonymous sender":goto rd.mail4
    input @2 \"Subject:" sb$:if sb$="" goto rd.mail4
    gosub editor:if not edit(2) goto rd.mail4
    print \edit(2)" bytes entered"
    print "Wait.." ;:h$="":s=8:gosub wr.ltr
    print ".reply sent":goto rd.mail2

wr.mail
    input @2 \"Filename (to write):" i$:if i$="" goto rd.mail4
    create i$:rewind:open #1,i$:input #7,i$
    append #1:copy #7,#1:close:goto rd.mail4

forward
    print \"Forward letter"
    a=d:gosub mail.who
    if d=0 then d=a:goto rd.mail4
    rewind:s=7
    input @2 "Subject:" sb$:if sb$="" sb$="For your information"
    h$="   --> A Forwarded Letter <--"
    r$=".letter forwarded":gosub snd.bulk
    d=a:goto rd.mail4

; send e-mail

snd.mail
```

```
        on nocar goto link.term
        print \"Send Mail"
        gosub mail.who:if d=0 return
        input @3 "Subject:" sb$:if sb$="" sb$="None"
        gosub editor:if not edit(2) return
        h$="":r$=".letter sent"
        s=8:goto snd.bulk

mail.who
        input @2 \"To who: Name, #, B)ulk mailing, <CR>):" i$
        clear #10:if i$="" then d=0:return
        if i$<>"B" gosub mail.wh2:print #10,d\0:return
        print \"Bulk Mailing":x=1
        y=5:if flag(2) then y=25

bulk1
        input @2 \"Send copy to (#,<CR>):" i$
        if i$="" then d=0:if x=1 return
        if i$<>"" gosub mail.wh2:if d=0 goto bulk1
        print #10,d:x=x+1:if d if x<y goto bulk1
        d=1:return

mail.wh2
        if left$(i$,1)="#" then i$=mid$(i$,2):goto snd.num
        if val(left$(i$,1)) goto snd.num
        d$=i$:if (d$="SYSOP") or (d$=sys$) then d=1:return
        if not instr(" ",i$) goto snd.usr2
        open #1,"b:users":d=1

snd.user
        position #1,128,d
        input #1,a$,b$\c$
        if (a$+" "+b$=d$) or (a$+b$=d$) close:return
        if d<nu then d=d+1:goto snd.user
        close:d=0
        print \d$" is not a user":return
snd.usr2
        print \"That user does not exist"
        d=0:return

snd.num
        d=val(i$)
        if (d<1) or (d>nu) goto snd.usr2
        move ram,58 to ram2:open #1,"b:users"
        position #1,128,d:input #1,a$,b$\c$
        position #1,128,d,70:read #1,ram,58
        close:i$=when$:move ram2,58 to ram
        if a$="" goto snd.usr2
        print \"Send to "c$\"Last on "i$;
        input @2 " ([Y]\N) ?" i$
        if left$(i$,1)="N" then d=0
```

```
        return

; write a bunch of letters to disk

snd.bulk
        print \edit(2)" bytes entered"
        print "Wait.." ;::mark(10)=0
snd.blk2
        input #10,d:if d=0 print r$:return
        gosub wr.ltr:print ".";::if s=7 rewind
        goto snd.blk2
; write the letter to disk

wr.ltr
        ready "g:mail"
        if info(6)<29 print \"Mail bit-map full":return
        print #msg(d),un:if h$<>"" print #6,h$\
        print #6,"Subj ->"sb$
        print #6,"From ->"a3$" (#"un")"
        print #6,"Date ->"date$" "time$\
        copy #s,#6:print #msg(d),chr$(4);chr$(0);
        msg(d)=1:update:return

; *** sub - routines ***

; backspace over text

backup
        print chr$(8,n);chr$(32,n);chr$(8,n);
        return

; enter a message

editor
        print \"Enter message now, "edit(3)" cols, [4k] max"
        print "[DONE] when finished, [.H] for help'
        cl=clock(2):clock(2)=0:edit(0):edit(1):clock(2)=cl:return

; show a disk file

show.file
        setint(1):print \s$\:open #1,f$:if mark(1) close #1:return
showfl2
        copy (20) #1
        if (eof(1) or key(1)) setint(""):close #1:return
        if not flag(35) goto showfl2
        print "Press [RETURN] ";::get i$:if i$=chr$(13) print " ";
        print chr$(8,16);chr$(32,16);chr$(8,16);
        if i$=" " setint(""):close #1:return
        setint(1):goto showfl2
```

System Segment – SYSTEM.SEG.S

```
; ******************
; GBBS "Pro" V:2.2
; Copyright 1986-2023
; Kevin M. Smallwood
; ******************
;
; system segment - 4/2/90

    on nocar goto term1

system
    x=(clock(2)-clock(1))/60:y=clock(2):x$=right$("0"+str$(x),2)
    if clock(1)>clock(2) x$="!!"
    if x=0 x$="--"
    if not y x$="**"
    if info(5) x$="::"
    print \"["x$"][System Level] ";
    input "Option (?=Help):" i$:push system
    if i$="L" goto log
    if i$="F" goto file
    if i$="R" goto request
    if i$="W" goto welcome
    if i$="D" goto dos.cmd
    if i$="N" goto new.user
    if i$="S" goto set.date
    if i$="T" goto terminate
    if i$="P" goto edit.pass
    if i$="K" goto kill.pass
    if i$="G" goto edit.file
    if i$="A" pop:link "a:main.seg","fromsys"
    if i$<>"?" print \"Illegal command":return

    setint(1):print sc$\s$\'
-----------------------------------
        List of supported commands:

A: Abort back    D: DOS commands
F: Read a file   G: Edit any file
K: Kill a user   L: The system log
N: Add new user  P: Edit any user
R: Read request  S: Set a new date
T: Terminate     W: Welcome update
----------------------------------':return


edit.pass
    input @2 \"Pass #" i$:if i$="" return
    a=val(i$):if i$="C" then a=un
```

```
ed.pass0
      if (a<1) or (a>nu) print \"No Such User":return
      d1$=a1$:d2$=a2$:d3$=a3$:d4$=a4$:d5$=a5$
      move ram,58 to ram2:if a<>un gosub rd.user
      if d1$<>"" goto ed.pass2
      input @2 \"No such user - create (Y/[N]) ?" i$
      if left$(i$,1)<>"Y" move ram2,58 to ram:return
ed.pass1
      fill ram,58,0:d1$="NEW":d2$="USER":
      d3$="New User":d4$="CITY":d5$="ST"
      pa$="PASSWORD":ph$="XXX-XXX-XXXX":nibble(5)=3

ed.pass2
      print \"A:"d3$\"B:"d4$", "d5$
      print "C:"a"-"pa$\"D:"ph$\"E:";
      for x=1 to 34:print flag(x);:next
      print \"F:"nibble(5)*10\"G:"when$
      input @2 \"Which (A-F):" i$

      if i$="A" input @3 \"Full Name:" d3$:gosub name.cov:goto ed.pass2
      if i$="B" input \"City:" d4$:input "State:" d5$:goto ed.pass2
      if i$="C" input \"Pass:" a$:pa$=left$(a$+"         ",8):goto
      ed.pass2
      if i$="D" input \"Phone:" a$:ph$=a$:goto ed.pass2
      if i$="F" input \"Time on:" x:nibble(5)=x/10
      if i$="" goto ed.pass5
      if i$<>"E" goto ed.pass2

      input @2 \"Lvl:" a$:if a$="" goto ed.pass2
      if a$="?" goto ed.pass3
      for x=1 to len(a$):if x>34 then x=len(a$)
      flag(x)=(mid$(a$,x,1)="1"):next:goto ed.pass2

ed.pass3
      open #1,"b:data2":for x=1 to 34
      position #1,32,x:input #1,a$:if a$="" goto ed.pass4
      print \a$\"Access (Y,N,S,Q):";:input @2 a$
      if a$="Q" then x=34
      if a$="Y" then flag(x)=1
      if a$="N" then flag(x)=0
ed.pass4
      next:close #1:goto ed.pass2

ed.pass5
      b=len(d1$+d2$+d4$+d5$):if b<32 goto ed.pass6
      print \"Name and City are too long."
      print "Max len=32, current len="b:goto ed.pass2

ed.pass6
      input @0 \"Save, Abort, or Return ?" i$
```

```
     if i$="A" move ram2,58 to ram:return
     if i$<>"S" goto ed.pass2
     if a>nu then nu=a
     if a=un then a1$=d1$:a2$=d2$:a3$=d3$:a4$=d4$:a5$=d5$:return
     gosub wr.user:move ram2,58 to ram:return

kill.pass
     input \"Kill #" a
     if (a<1) or (a>nu) return
     move ram,58 to ram2:gosub rd.user
     a$=mid$(" "+when$,2)
     if d1$="" print \"That user does not exist":move ram2,58 to
     ram:return
     print \"Kill "d3$\"Last on "a$;
     input @0 " ?" i$
     if i$<>"Y" move ram2,58 to ram:return
     d1$="":gosub wr.user
     print \"User Killed"
     move ram2,58 to ram:return

request
     print \"Read Request File":open #2,"b:request"
     if mark(2) close:print \"File empty":return
     input @2 \"Send file to printer (Y/[N]) ?" i$
     if i$="Y" setint(1):copy #2,#5:mark(2)=0
req2
     input #2,a:b=mark(2):if a goto req3
     close:input @0 \"Delete File ?" i$:if i$="Y" kill "b:request"
     return
req3
     mark(2)=b:print \md$
req3a
     input #2,i$:if i$<>chr$(1) print i$:goto req3a
     print md$
req4
     input @2 \"Request [V, K, C, R, A, Q]:" i$
     if i$="R" goto req3
     if i$="Q" close:return
     if i$="C" or i$="" goto req2
     if i$="K" then d1$="":gosub wr.user:goto req2
     if i$="V" gosub ed.pass0:goto req2
     if i$<>"A" goto req4
     print \"Enter message now, "edit(3)" col, 4k bytes max"
     print 'Type "DONE" when finished ".h" for help'
     edit(0):edit(1):if not edit(2) goto req4
     print \"Wait...";:x=mark(2):close:ready "g:mail"
     print #msg(a),1\"From ->"a3$" (#1)"
     print #6,"Date ->"date$" "time$\:copy #8,#6
     print #msg(a),chr$(4);chr$(0);:msg(a)=1:update
     open #2,"b:request":mark(2)=x
     print ".Letter sent":goto req4
```

```
file
     input @2 \"File Name (to read):" i$
     f$=i$:if i$="" return
     input @2 \"Show file on printer (Y/[N]) ?" i$
     if i$<>"Y" goto show.file
     setint(1):copy f$,#5:return

log
     input @0 \"Log: D)elete, S)how, P)rint, Q)uit ?" i$
     if i$="D" kill "b:log.system":return
     if i$="S" f$="b:log.system":gosub show.file
     if i$="P" setint(1):copy "b:log.system",#5:setint("")
     if (i$="A") or (i$="Q") return
     goto log

terminate
     print \"Terminate Connection"
     input @2 \"Are you sure (Y/[N]) ?" i$
     if left$(i$,1)<>"Y" return
term1
     link "a:main.seg","termin2"

welcome
     print \"Show current welcome to all users ([Y]/N) ?";
     input @2 i$:if left$(i$,1)="N" return
     wm=mn:mn=mn+1:print \"News updated":return

edit.file
     print \"Edit a File"
     input @2 \"File Name (to load):" i$
     edit(0):if i$<>"" copy i$,#8
     print \"Enter/Edit File Now: "edit(3)" cols, 4k max"
     print 'Type "DONE" when finished ".h" for help'
     edit(1):if not edit(2) return
     input @2 \"File Name (to save):" i$
     if i$="" return
     kill i$:create i$:open #1,i$
     copy #8,#1:close:return

dos.cmd
     input @2 \"DOS:" i$:if i$="" return
     use "b:xdos",i$:return

new.user
     input @0 \"Add a new user (Y/[N]) ?" i$
     if left$(i$,1)<>"Y" return
     move ram,58 to ram2
     a=nu+1:goto ed.pass1
```

```
set.date
    print \"Current date: "date$
    input @2 \"Today's Date: "i$:date$=i$
    print \"New date: "date$:return

; *** sub-routines ***

rd.user
    open #1,"b:users"
    position #1,128,a
    input #1,d1$,d2$\d3$\d4$,d5$
    position #1,128,a,70
    read #1,ram,58
    close #1
    return

wr.user
    open #1,"b:users":position #1,128,a
    if d1$="" then d1$="":d2$=""
    print #1,d1$","d2$\d3$\d4$","d5$
    position #1,128,a,70
    write #1,ram,58:close #1
    if d1$="" ready "g:mail":kill #msg(a):update
    return

show.file
    setint(1):print \s$\:copy f$:return

name.cov
    i$=d3$:a$="":for l=1 to len(i$)
    x=asc(mid$(i$,l,1)):if x>96 then x=x-32
    a$=a$+chr$(x):next:x=instr(" ",a$)
    if not(x) d2$=a$:d1$=".":return
    d1$=left$(a$,x-1):d2$=mid$(a$,x+1)
    return
```

Bulletin Copy Utility – BC.S

```
;  *******************
;  GBBS Pro v2.2
;  Copyright 1986-2023
;  Kevin M. Smallwood
;  *******************

;  Bulletin Copy Utility
;  By GS @ 04/30/85
;  Modified by Lance @ 4/20/87
;  Updated for 2.1 - 04/11/90
;  Updated for 2.2 - 02/19/17

     public start

     input "press [ret] to continue..." i$

     flag=ram
     s1$="<"+chr$(8):s2$=">"+chr$(8)
     s3$="{"+chr$(8):s4$="}"+chr$(8)

start
     home
     print "Bulletin Copy Utility v2.2"
     print \"Written by Greg Schaefer"
     print "Modified for v2.2 by BillM"
     input \"Source Bulletin File (ex: F:B1):" f1$
     open #1,f1$:a=mark(1):close
     if a print \"Cant find "f1$" press [RET] ";:get i$:goto start
     ready f1$:print chr$(8);:sz=(peek(36)=79)
     fill ram,64,0:if msg(0) goto status
     print \"That message file is empty."
     gosub getret:goto start

status
     home:z=1:b=(msg(0)/20)*5+1
     for x=1 to b step 5
     a=20:if x=b a=msg(0) mod 20
     for y=5 to a+4:a$=left$("*",flag(z))
     print @x,y      ;z;a$;::z=z+1:next:next

cmd
     print @1,1 "R=Restart, Q=Quit, V=View, C=Copy"
     print "K=Kill, T=Tag, U=Untag, W=Write"
     print "Enter Cmd: ";chr$(32,28);chr$(8,28);
     get i$:if i$>"a" i$=chr$(asc(i$)-32)
     print chr$(8)  ;i$;::z=1
     if i$="Q" goto quit
```

```
      if i$="V" goto view
      if i$="C" goto copy
      if i$="K" goto kill
      if i$="T" goto tag
      if i$="U" goto untag
      if i$="R" goto restart
      if i$="W" goto write
      goto cmd

quit
      input @0 "uit Y/N ?" i$:if i$<>"Y" goto cmd
      home:goto doquit

restart
      input @0 "estart Y/N ?" i$:if i$<>"Y" goto cmd
      home:goto start

tag
      input @2 "ag (#[,#] or ALL):" i$
      if i$="" goto cmd
      if left$(i$,1)="A" fill ram,64,255:goto status
tag2
      a=val(i$):if not ((a=0) or (a>msg(0))) flag(a)=1
      a=instr(",",i$):if a i$=mid$(i$,a+1):goto tag2
      goto status

untag
      input @2 "ntag (#[,#] or ALL):" i$
      if i$="" goto cmd
      if left$(i$,1)="A" fill ram,64,0:goto status
untag2
      a=val(i$):if not ((a=0) or (a>msg(0))) flag(a)=0
      a=instr(",",i$):if a i$=mid$(i$,a+1):goto untag2
      goto status

view
      input @2 "iew (ALL,TAG,#[,#]):" i$
      gosub inprng:if i$="" goto cmd
      home:print "Viewing Bulletin(s):"
view2
      d=0:gosub show:if a goto view2
      gosub getret:goto status

write
      input @2 "rite (ALL,TAG,#[,#]):" i$
      gosub inprng:if i$="" goto cmd
write2
      home:print "Write these bulletins:"\
      gosub list:input @2 \"Filename (to write):" f$
      if f$="" goto cmd
```

```
     create f$:open #1,f$:append #1
     print \"Wait...Writing bulletin(s)"
write3
     d=1:gosub show:if a goto write3
     close:goto status

kill
     input @2 "ill (ALL,TAG,#[,#]):" i$
     gosub inprng:if i$="" goto cmd
     home:print "Kill these bulletins:"\:gosub list
     input @0 \"Kill: Are you sure Y/N ?" i$
     if i$<>"Y" goto status
     print "Wait...Killing bulletin(s)"
     b=msg(msg(0)):for x=1 to msg(0)
     if flag(x+512) kill #msg(x)
     next:crunch:a=msg(0):if a msg(a)=b
     update:if a goto status
     home:print \"All bulletins killed."
     gosub getret:goto start

copy
     input @2 "opy (ALL,TAG,#[,#]):" i$
     gosub inprng:if i$="" goto cmd
     home:print "Copy these bulletins:"\:gosub list
     input @0 \"Copy: Are you sure Y/N ?" i$
     if i$<>"Y" goto status
copy2
     print \"Enter destination bulletin file"
     input @2 \"Destin Bulletin File (ex: D:B2):" f$
     if f$="" goto cmd
     open #1,f$:a=mark(1):close:b=msg(0)
     if a print "Can't find "f$" press [RET]";:get i$:goto copy2
     print \"Wait...Copying bulletin(s): ";
     open #1,"b:data":input #1,c1,c2,ct,ct$,da$
     input #1,nu,mn,wm\lu$:close:ready f$

     for x=1 to b:if not flag(x+512) goto copy3
     print s1$        ;:kill "dummy":create "dummy":open #1,"dummy"
     print s2$        ;:ready f1$:copy #msg(x),#1:close:ready f$
     print s3$        ;:b=msg(0)+1:copy "dummy",#msg(b):msg(b)=mn
     update:mn=mn+1:print s4$;
copy3
     next:open #1,"b:data":print #1,c1,c2,ct,ct$,da$
     print #1,nu,mn,wm\lu$:close:ready f1$:goto status

inprng
     if left$(i$,1)="T" move ram,64 to ram2:return
     if left$(i$,1)="A" fill ram2,64,255:return
     fill ram2,64,0
```

```
inprng2
    a=val(i$):if (a=0) or (a>msg(0)) i$="":return
    flag(a+512)=1:a=instr(",",i$):if not a return
    i$=mid$(i$,a+1):goto inprng2

list
    a$="":for x=1 to msg(0)
    if flag(x+512) print a$x;:a$=","
    next:if peek(36)>0 print
    return

show
    if z>msg(0) a=0:return
    if flag(z+512)=0 z=z+1:goto show
    input #msg(z),sb$\b,b$\c,c$
    print #d,\"Numb ->"z" of "msg(0)\" Sub ->"sb$
    print #d, "  To ->"b$\"From ->"c$
    copy #6,#d:a=1:z=z+1:return

getret
    input @2 \"Press [RETURN] to continue... "i$
    return

doquit
    end
```

Message File Converter – MSG.CONVERT.S

```
; ******************
; GBBS "Pro" V:2.2
; Copyright 1986-2023
; Kevin M. Smallwood
; ******************
; Message File 1.0-1.2 to 2.2 Converter
; This module will convert the stock GBBS Pro V:1.2
; message formats to the standard V:2.2 format.
; *NOTE*: If you have modified your message segments
; to alter the way it writes the header info you will
; need to adjust this program accordingly.

; Written by Lance on 02/03/87
; Updated to 2.1 on 04/11/90 - LPT
; Updated to 2.2 on 02/19/17 - WPM

msg.conv
     print '
Once this program runs your message
files will be in V:2.1 format and will
not run under 1.0-1.2.  Once you do this
there is no turnning back.'
     print \"Do you wish to continue (YES/[NO]) ? NO";
     print chr$(8,2);:input i$
     if i$<>"YES" end

     open #1,"b:data2"
     mark(1)=1120:input #1,ab
     close
     print \"System has "ab" sub-boards"\
     for bb=1 to ab
     gosub read.msg
     print "Converting Board #"bb" - The "bn$
     print "Message #";
     for a=1 to msg(0)
     print a          ;
     edit(0):gosub convert
     print chr$(8,(len(str$(a))));
     next:print:print:next
     print '
Conversion complete!

Your systems Message files are now
converted to run under GBBS Pro V:2.2

Please make sure you have made the
changes to your message segments
```

```
before running the board with the
messages in this format.':end

read.msg
    open #1,"b:data2":position #1,128,bb+8
    input #1,bn$\bf$\b3,b4\bs,bs$\mb,kl,kb
    close:ready bf$
    return

convert
    input #msg(a),un,sb$\fr$
    copy #6,#8
    ti=0:ti$="All Users"
    x=msg(a):kill #msg(a)
    print #msg(a),sb$\ti,ti$\un,mid$(fr$,8)
    copy #8,#6:msg(a)=x:update
    return
```

New Message Fix – NEW.MSG.FIX.S

```
; ******************
;  GBBS "Pro" V:2.2
;  New Msg Fix
; Copyright 1986-2023
; Kevin M. Smallwood
; ******************
    byte=ram

start
    text:home
    print "New Msg Fix V2.2"
    print \"Reset users to see all or none of"
    print "the new bulletins?"
    input @0 \"(All/None):" i$
    if i$="A" lr=1
    if i$="N" lr=2
    if not lr goto start
    open #1,"b:data"
    input #1,c1,c2,ct,ct$,da$
    input #1,nu,mn,wm,tm\lu$
    close:mn=1:tm=0
    bb=1:gosub bl.ld1nf
    for x=1 to ab
    bb=x:gosub bl.ldinf
    print \"Fixing: "bn$
    ready bf$
```

```
      if not msg(0) goto loop
      for y=1 to msg(0)
      msg(y)=mn:mn=mn+1
      tm=tm+1:next

loop
      next:update
      if lr=2 then lr=mn

      print \"Fixing Users..."\
      open #1,"b:users"
      for x=1 to nu
      print "Fixing user #"x" of "nu;:poke 36,0
      position #1,128,x
      input #1,a$
      if a$="" goto loop2

      byte(0)=lr mod 256:byte(1)=lr/256
      position #1,128,x,112
      write #1,ram,2

loop2
      next:close

      open #1,"b:data"
      print #1,c1,c2,ct,ct$,da$
      print #1,nu,mn,wn,tm\lu$
      close

      print \\"New Msg Fix Complete"
      end

bl.ldinf
      if bb=0 then bf$="":bl=0:return
      me=0:if bl=bb ready bf$:return
      bl=bb:open #1,"b:data2"
      mark(1)=1120:input #1,ab
      if bb>ab close:bf$="":bl=0:return
      position #1,128,bb+8
      input #1,bn$\bf$\b3,b4\bs,bs$\mb,kl,kb
      b1=1:if b3 then b1=flag(b3)
      b2=1:if b4 then b2=flag(b4)
      close:if bf$="" then bl=0:return
      if (b1) ready bf$:nn=nb
      return
```

User Converter – USER.CONVERT.S

```
; ******************
; GBBS "Pro" V:2.2
; Copyright 1986-2023
; Kevin M. Smallwood
; ******************
; 12/23/86  By Lance
; 04/11/90  Updated to 2.1 - LPT
; 02/19/2017 Updated to 2.2 - WPM
; Get data from the Data file for number of users to convert

user.conv
     print '
This program will convert your 1.2 user
file to run under the 2.2 format.  It
will not harm your existing user file.':print
     print \"Do you wish to continue (YES/[NO]) ? NO";
     print chr$(8,2):input i$
     if i$<>"YES" end

rd.data
     open #1,"b:data"
     input #1,c1,c2,ct,ct$,da$
     input #1,nu,mn,wm,tm\lu$:close
     print "System has "nu" users"\

; Start the actual conversion
; create the temp user file

     create "b:users.temp"
     open #1,"b:users"
     open #2,"b:users.temp"
     print "Converting User #";
     for x=1 to nu:print x;

; set the ram for the old file

     set pa$=ram,8:set ph$=ram+8,12
     when$=ram+20:flag=ram+22
     nibble=ram+27:byte=ram+29
     gosub rd.old.user
     d$=d1$+" "+d2$:gosub cn.name:d3$=xx$

; Save the stats for conversion to the new format

     tl=nibble(1):ct=nibble(2):up=nibble(3)
     tc=byte(0):bp=byte(1):dl=byte(2)
     lm=byte(3):hm=byte(4):wh$=when$:z=flag
```

```
; Set up the new 128 byte ram area

     set pa$=ram,8:set ph$=ram+8,12
     when$=ram+20:flag=ram+22
     nibble=ram+27:byte=ram+37

; Give all users zero nulls & convert the number of uploads

     for l=1 to 4:nibble(l)=0:next
     nibble(5)=tl:nibble(6)=ct:byte(1)=tc
     byte(2)=bp:byte(3)=dl:byte(4)=ul
     byte(5)=lm:byte(6)=hm:byte(0)=0
     when$=wh$:flag=z:d4$="":d5$=""
     gosub wr.new.user

     print chr$(8,(len(str$(x))));
     next:close

; Rename the files so that 2.2 will run. (saving 1.2's file)

     use "b:xdos","r b:users,b:users.1.2"
     use "b:xdos","r b:users.temp,b:users"
     print "System is now ready for 2.1":end

rd.old.user
     position #1,64,x
     input #1,d1$,d2$\d3$
     position #1,64,x,30
     read #1,ram,34:return

wr.new.user
     position #2,128,x
     print #2,d1$,d2$\d3$\d4$,d5$
     position #2,128,x,70
     write #2,ram,58:return

cn.name
     xx$="":for y=2 to len(d$)
     q$=mid$(d$,y,1):if q$=" " q$=mid$(d$,y,2):y=y+1:goto cn.name2
     if q$="." q$=mid$(d$,y,2):y=y+1:goto cn.name2
     if q$="-" q$=mid$(d$,y,2):y=y+1:goto cn.name2
     if q$="_" q$=mid$(d$,y,2):y=y+1:goto cn.name2
     if q$=" " q$=mid$(d$,y,2):y=y+1:goto cn.name2
     a=asc(q$):if (a<65) or (a>91) and (a<97) y=y+1:goto cn.name2
     a=a+32:q$=chr$(a)
cn.name2
     xx$=xx$+q$:next:xx$=left$(d$,1)+xx$:return
```

APPENDICES

ASCII Character Chart

DEC	HEX	CHAR	KEY	DEC	HEX	CHAR	KEY
00	00	NULL	Ctrl-@	31	1F	US	_
01	01	SOH	Ctrl-A	32	20	SPC	
02	02	STX	Ctrl-B	33	21	!	!
03	03	ETX	Ctrl-C	34	22	"	"
04	04	ET	Ctrl-D	35	23	#	#
05	05	ENQ	Ctrl-E	36	24	$	$
06	06	ACK	Ctrl-F	37	25	%	%
07	07	BEL	Ctrl-G	38	26	&	&
08	08	BS	Ctrl-H	39	27	'	'
09	09	HT	Ctrl-I	40	28	(	(
10	0A	LF	Ctrl-J	41	29	)	)
11	0B	VT	Ctrl-K	42	2A	*	*
12	0C	FF	Ctrl-L	43	2B	+	+
13	0D	CR	RETURN	44	2C	,	,
14	0E	SO	Ctrl-N	45	2D	-	-
15	0F	SI	Ctrl-O	46	2E	.	.
16	10	DLF	Ctrl-P	47	2F	/	/
17	11	DC1	Ctrl-Q	48	30	0	0
18	12	DC2	Ctrl-R	49	31	1	1
19	13	DC3	Ctrl-S	50	32	2	2
20	14	DC4	Ctrl-T	51	33	3	3
21	15	NAK	Ctrl-U	52	34	4	4
22	16	SYN	Ctrl-V	53	35	5	5
23	17	ETB	Ctrl-W	54	36	6	6
24	18	CAN	Ctrl-X	55	37	7	7
25	19	EM	Ctrl-Y	56	38	8	8
26	1A	SUB	Ctrl-Z	57	39	9	9
27	1B	ESC	ESCAPE	58	3A	:	:
28	1C	FS	Ctrl-\	59	3B	;	;
29	1D	GS	Ctrl-]	60	3C	<	<
30	1E	RS	Ctrl-^	61	3D	=	=

DEC	HEX	CHAR	KEY	DEC	HEX	CHAR	KEY
62	3E	>	>	95	5F	_	_
63	3F	?	?	96	60	`	`
64	40	@	@	97	61	a	a
65	41	A	A	98	62	b	b
66	42	B	B	99	63	c	c
67	43	C	C	100	64	d	d
68	44	D	D	101	65	e	e
69	45	E	E	102	66	f	f
70	46	F	F	103	67	g	g
71	47	G	G	104	68	h	h
72	48	H	H	105	69	i	i
73	49	I	I	106	6A	j	j
74	4A	J	J	107	6B	k	k
75	4B	K	K	108	6C	l	l
76	4C	L	L	109	6D	m	m
77	4D	M	M	110	6E	n	n
78	4E	N	N	111	6F	o	o
79	4F	O	O	112	70	p	p
80	50	P	P	113	71	q	q
81	51	Q	Q	114	72	r	r
82	52	R	R	115	73	s	s
83	53	S	S	116	74	t	t
84	54	T	T	117	75	u	u
85	55	U	U	118	76	v	v
86	56	V	V	119	77	w	w
87	57	W	W	120	78	x	x
88	58	X	X	121	79	y	y
89	59	Y	Y	122	7A	z	z
90	5A	Z	Z	123	7B	{	{
91	5B	[	[	124	7C	|	|
92	5C	\	\	125	7D	}	}
93	5D	]	]	126	7E	~	~
94	5E	^	^	127	7F	DEL	DEL

Modem / RS-232 Selection And Hookup

GBBS Pro actually supports more modems and serial cards than
are listed in the software itself. This is because some newer or lesser
known hardware is completely compatible with the more familiar
standards listed in the CONFIG program. For example, the Videx
PSIO interface card operates as an Apple Super Serial Card. If you
had a Videx PSIO, then you could tell CONFIG that you had an
Apple SSC in that slot and it wouldn't know the difference! If your
card is not listed, then check your manual and see if it says that it's
compatible with one of the supported cards.

RS-232 And Modem Compatibility

You might need to give special attention to the way your modem
is connected to your computer. If you have a single-speed modem,
then you may use most any "straight" cable. To get a single speed
modem to work, you need the following pins to be hooked up: 2, 3,
7, 8, 20. Generally, pins 4 and 5 are also hooked up, but this can vary
depending on the modem.

There are several ways of hooking up multiple-speed modems.
The hookup varies from modem to modem. The following list shows
how to hookup many of the popular modems out on the market. If you
cannot find your modem listed, then look for a "compatible" modem if
one exists. Generally, most modems will work, with the exception of
the Apple Personal Modem.

Apple Modem 1200 – Use cable #4. Configure as Apple Modem
1200. Set switches: All Up.

Hayes Smartmodem 1200 – Use cable #2. Configure as
Smartmodem 1200. Set switches: 1-Up, 2-n/a, 3-n/a, 4-n/a, 5-Up,
6-Up, 7-n/a, 8-Down

Hayes Smartmodem 2400 – Use cable #3. Configure as Smartmodem 2400. Use a terminal program, enter the command "AT&C1&D2&W" to set the modem to respond to DTR and not to override DCD. Save these settings into NOVRAM.

Novation Smartcat Plus – Use cable #3. Configure as Smartcat Plus. Set switches: 1-Off, 2-On, 3-Off, 4-On, 5-On, 6-Off, 7-On, 8-On. It has been reported that you can also use cable #1, though this is not confirmed.

Novation Professional 2400 – Use cable #3. Configure as Professional 2400. Set switches: A1-Off, A2-On, A3-Off, A7-On, A8-On, B3-On

Prentice Popcorn X100 – Use cable #2. No switches.

Prometheus Promodem 1200 – Use cable #1. Configure as Promodem 1200. Set switches: 1-On, 2-On, 3-Off, 4-Off, 5-Off, 6-On, 7-Off, 8-Off, 9-Off, 10-Off.

Prometheus Promodem 1200A – No cable needed. Configure as Promodem 1200. Set switches: 1-Off, 2-Off, 3-Off, 4-n/a, 5-n/a, 6-n/a.

US Robotics Auto-Dial 212A – Use cable #2. Configure as Smartmodem 1200. Set switches: Unknown.

US Robotics Password – Use cable #1. Configure as Password. Set switches: All Up.

US Robotics Courier 2400 – Use cable #3. Configure as Courier 2400. Set switches: 1-Off, 3-Off, 6-Off.

Generic Multiple Speed Modem

Almost any multiple speed modem can be made to work with *GBBS Pro*. It is just a matter of how smoothly it runs. With the generic multiple speed modem driver, a caller must press RETURN a few times so that the board can detect the baud rate they are calling with and "sync-in" with the caller. This is what is called a "manual-syncing driver". All the other drivers are "automatic-syncing drivers".

Generic Multiple Speed Modem 300/1200 – Use cable #4. Configure as Multiple Speed Driver 300/1200. Set switches: Set so that it responds to DTR, autoanswers the phone, and returns the status of Carrier Detect.

Generic Multiple Speed Modem 300/2400 – Use cable #4. Configure as Multiple Speed Driver 300/2400. Set switches: Set so that it responds to DTR, autoanswers the phone, and returns the status of Carrier Detect.

Generic No Carrier Modem

There are a small group of modems that due to an oversight by the manufacturers do not support Carrier Detect. Meaning you can't actually ever tell if there is a remote modem connected. This makes it difficult to support this type of modem since this is a very important function of a bulletin board.

However, a partial solution has been provided in the form of the "No Carrier 300" and "No Carrier 1200" drivers. These modems must be fully Hayes compatible. To use this driver with either a modem that does not support Carrier Detect or with a cable that does not, just select the correct driver for your modem's speed.

RS-232 Cable Charts

RS-232		MODEM

Cable #1: 2,3,4,5   -->   2,3,4,5

6,7,8,20   -->   6,7,8,20

Cable #2: 2,3,4,5   -->   2,3,4,5

6   -->   12

7,8,20   -->   7,8,20

Cable #3: 2,3,4,5   -->   2,3,4,5

6   -->   8

7   -->   7

8 & 20   -->   20

There is a 3-way connection between Pins 8 and 20 of the RS-232
and Pin 20 of the modem.

Cable #4: 2   -->   9

3   -->   5

4 & 5

6   -->   2

7   -->   3

8   -->   7

20   -->   6

The modem end is a DIN-9 connector for the Apple modem.

Cable #5: Apple IIc and Laser

1	-->	20
2	-->	7
3	-->	8
4	-->	2
5	-->	3
		4 & 5

The 5-pin DIN is numbered in DIN-5 format, not Apple format. Pins 4 and 5 on the modem side are jumpered.

Cable #10:

1	-->	20
2	-->	6 & 8
3	-->	2
4 & 8	-->	7
5	-->	3

There is a 3-way connection between Pins 6 and 8 of the modem and Pin 2 of the RS-232 and a 3-way connection between Pins 4 and 8 of the RS-232 and Pin 7 of the modem.

Other Modems

If your modem is not listed as a usable modem, but it supports Auto-Answer, then you can probably use it with *GBBS Pro*. First you must get a cable that supports the following pins: TD, RD, GND, CD, DTR.

If you are using a 300/1200 modem then it needs to support the HS (high speed) line. The HS pin if used must be connected to DSR on the RS-232. To make your modem work, you must set its switches (or it must default) to the following operating conditions:

1. Auto-answer phone when DTR is high.

2. Use DTR (not override it).

3. Use TRUE CARRIER DETECT (not override it).

4. Not respond to any commands sent to it by the computer. If it is a smart-type modem and takes commands, then disable command recognition.

5. Hang up/reset upon loss of DTR.

Once you have set your modem to work with the following conditions, select either "300 Baud Modem" or "Smartmodem 1200" from config.

A Note to Apple IIc Owners

The only drivers that you can use are the multi-speed drivers or the standard 300 baud. This is due to the lack of a speed pin on the Apple IIc modem port. Standard Serial Cables may be used using the "No Carrier SSC Driver" but you may have mixed results.

VT-100 Control Sequences

Complete VT-100 Control Sequences, not including device specific codes, are useful in *GBBS*. These are not supported on the local screen. ACOS doesn't support any emulations – you can't give it a command that then outputs an emulation sequence. However, if a message (text or message uploaded to the editor) is already set up with emulation sequences in them, *ACOS/GBBS* will send them out. The codes are provided so users can create their own custom screens.

(	Font Set G0	<ESC>(
0	Set G0 special characters & line set	<ESC>(0
1	Set G0 alternate character ROM	<ESC>(1
2	Set G0 alt char ROM and special graphics	<ESC>(2
A	Set United Kingdom G0 character set	<ESC>(A
B	Set United States G0 character set	<ESC>(B
)	Font Set G1	<ESC>)
0	Set G1 special characters & line set	<ESC>)0
1	Set G1 alternate character ROM	<ESC>)1
2	Set G1 alt char ROM and special graphics	<ESC>)2
A	Set United Kingdom G1 character set	<ESC>)A
B	Set United States G1 character set	<ESC>)B
=	Set alternate keypad mode	<ESC>=
>	Set numeric keypad mode	<ESC>>
3	Double-height letters, top half	<ESC>#3
4	Double-height letters, bottom half	<ESC>#4
5	Single width, single height letters	<ESC>#5
6	Double width, single height letters	<ESC>#6

8	Screen alignment display	`<ESC>#8`
7	Save cursor position and attributes	`<ESC>7`
8	Restore cursor position and attributes	`<ESC>8`
D	Move/scroll window up one line	`<ESC>D`
E	Move to next line	`<ESC>E`
H	Set a tab at the current column	`<ESC>H`
M	Move/scroll window down one line	`<ESC>M`
N	Set single shift 2	`<ESC>N`
O	Set single shift 3	`<ESC>O`
c	Reset terminal to initial state	`<ESC>c`
n	Response: terminal is OK	`<ESC>0n`
n	Response: terminal is not OK	`<ESC>3n`
n	Device status report	`<ESC>5n`
n	Get cursor position	`<ESC>6n`
A	Move cursor up n lines	`<ESC>[ValueA`
B	Move cursor down n lines	`<ESC>[ValueB`
C	Move cursor right n lines	`<ESC>[ValueC`
D	Move cursor left n lines	`<ESC>[ValueD`
H	Move cursor to screen location v,h (no parameters is 0,0)	`<ESC>[Line;ColumnH`
J	Clear screen from cursor down	`<ESC>[J`
J	Clear screen from cursor down	`<ESC>[0J`
J	Clear screen from cursor up	`<ESC>[1J`
J	Clear entire screen	`<ESC>[2J`

K	Clear line from cursor right	`<ESC>[K`
K	Clear line from cursor right	`<ESC>[0K`
K	Clear line from cursor left	`<ESC>[1K`
K	Clear entire line	`<ESC>[2K`
R	Response: cursor is at v,h	`<ESC>Line;ColumnR`
c	Identify what terminal type	`<ESC>[c`
c	Identify what terminal type (another)	`<ESC>[0c`
c	Report Device Code	`<ESC>[{code}0c`
c	Response: terminal type code n	`<ESC>[?1;Value0c`
f	Move cursor to upper left corner	`<ESC>[f`
f	Move cursor to upper left corner	`<ESC>[;f`
f	Move cursor to screen location v,h	`<ESC>[Line;Columnf`
g	Clear and Reset Tabs (see below)	`<ESC>[{#};{#};{#}g`
h	Set cursor key to application	`<ESC>[1h`
h	Set number of columns to 132	`<ESC>[3h`
h	Set smooth scrolling	`<ESC>[4h`
h	Set reverse video on screen	`<ESC>[5h`
h	Set origin to relative	`<ESC>[6h`
h	Set auto-wrap mode	`<ESC>[7h`
h	Set auto-repeat mode	`<ESC>[8h`
h	Set interlacing mode	`<ESC>[9h`
h	Set new line mode	`<ESC>[20h`

i	Print Screen	`<ESC>[i`
i	Print Line	`<ESC>[1i`
i	Stop Print Log	`<ESC>[4i`
i	Start Print Log	`<ESC>[5i`

l	Set cursor key to cursor	`<ESC>[1l`
l	Set VT52 (versus ANSI)	`<ESC>[2l`
l	Set number of columns to 80	`<ESC>[3l`
l	Set jump scrolling	`<ESC>[4l`
l	Set normal video on screen	`<ESC>[5l`
l	Set origin to absolute	`<ESC>[6l`
l	Reset auto-wrap mode	`<ESC>[7l`
l	Reset auto-repeat mode	`<ESC>[8l`
l	Reset interlacing mode	`<ESC>[9l`
l	Set line feed mode	`<ESC>[20l`

m	Set Display Attributes (see below)	`<ESC>[#;#;#m`
m	Turn off character attributes	`<ESC>[m`
m	Turn off character attributes	`<ESC>[0m`
m	Turn bold mode on	`<ESC>[1m`
m	Turn low intensity mode on	`<ESC>[2m`
m	Turn underline mode on	`<ESC>[4m`
m	Turn blinking mode on	`<ESC>[5m`
m	Turn reverse video on	`<ESC>[7m`
m	Turn invisible text mode on	`<ESC>[8m`

n	Report Device OK	`<ESC>[0n`
n	Report Device Failure	`<ESC>[3n`
n	Query Device Status	`<ESC>[5n`
n	Query Cursor Position	`<ESC>[6n`
p	Set Key Definition	`<ESC>[{key};"{string}"p`
q	Turn off all four LEDs	`<ESC>[0q`
q	Turn on LED #1	`<ESC>[1q`
q	Turn on LED #2	`<ESC>[2q`
q	Turn on LED #3	`<ESC>[3q`
q	Turn on LED #4	`<ESC>[4q`
r	Set top/bottom lines of window to full size	`<ESC>[Line;Liner` (no parameters)
s	Save Cursor	`<ESC>[s`
u	Restore Cursor	`<ESC>[u`
y	Confidence power up test	`<ESC>[2;1y`
y	Confidence loopback test	`<ESC>[2;2y`
y	Repeat power up test	`<ESC>[2;9y`
y	Repeat loopback test	`<ESC>[2;10y`

Tab Control Position

1   Clear code
2   Set horizontal tab count (every n spaces)
3   Set vertical tab count (every n lines)

Tab Clear Control Codes

0   Clear current horizontal, default
1   Clear current vertical
2   Clear all
3   Clear all horizontal
4   Clear all vertical

Display Attributes

0   Reset attributes
1   Bright
2   Dim
4   Underscore
5   Blink
7   Reverse
8   Hidden
30   Text Black
31   Text Red
32   Text Green
33   Text Yellow
34   Text Blue
35   Text Magenta
36   Text Cyan
37   Text White
40   Back Black
41   Back Red
42   Back Green
43   Back Yellow
44   Back Blue
45   Back Magenta
46   Back Cyan
47   Back White

Building *GBBS Pro* From Source Code

These instructions detail how to build *GBBS Pro* 2.x from source code in *Merlin 8/16* on a IIGS running GS/OS. *GBBS Pro* disk images and source code are available from the official Web site: https://gbbs.applearchives.com. Before you start, setup your source code in a directory on your IIGS similar to:

```
WORK/GBBS/CONFIG
        /ACOS
        /GBBS.CONFIG
        /GBBS.SYSTEM
```

Copy the "Config" sources to the config folder, the "ACOS" sources to the ACOS folder, and the files from the GBBS Config floppy to the GBBS.CONFIG folder, and the files from the GBBS system floppy to the GBBS.SYSTEM folder.

Config and ACOS are where you will be editing, assembling and linking source code. Once you are ready to test a build, copy the resulting files from /Config to /GBBS.CONFIG and the resulting files from /ACOS to /GBBS.SYSTEM. Then copy the contents of the /GBBS folders to floppy disks images (.DSK or .PO) for testing in a virtual machine. Those images can later be written to actual floppy disks (e.g., via Applesauce) for use on real hardware.

Build Steps

1. You may need to edit your *Merlin 8/16* PARMS file to match on the following defines, then assemble the file to create a new PARMS file:

```
BUB              DFB    %01100110
LSTDODFT         DFB    %01001001
```

2. Use the NEWPARMS command to load the new PARMS file:

    `NEWPARMS`

3. Set prefix 2 to your *GBBS Pro* folder:

    `PFX 2=/DRIVE/GBBS.SOURCE`

    Create a project with the PROJECT command:

    `PROJECT SAVE GBBS`

    If you save a GBBS project, be sure to use the NEWPARMS
    command before saving, as the params are part of the project! This
    is great, because then you can restore the default params settings
    and only have the GBBS params applied when working on the
    GBBS project.

4. Change your prefix to the CONFIG folder:

    `PFX 2/CONFIG`

5. Load and assemble all the files in these folders (yes, one at a time).
    You will want to use the PFX command to change the current
    directory to the base for each of these sub-folders, like
    PFX 2/CONFIG/CLOCKS.

    ```
    CLOCKS/
            IIC
            IIGS
            MOUNTAIN
            NO.SLOT
            NULL
            PRODOS
            SERIALPRO
            THUNDER
            ULTRA
            VERSA
    ```

```
MODEMS/
            CAT103
            CAT212
            GSPORT      (TWICE, 1st for Slot 1, 2nd for Slot 2)
            GSPORT.HST  (TWICE, 1st for Slot 1, 2nd for Slot 2)
            HAYES.NEW   (TWICE, 1st for Slot 1, 2nd for Slot 2)
            HAYES.SSC   (Super Serial Card)
            MM2
            MULTISPD
            NOCAR
            NULLMDM
            SINGLESPD

    PRINTERS/
            NULL
            PARALLEL
            SERIAL
            GRAPPLER

    VIDEO/
            VID40
            VID40PL
            VID80
            VIDEX
```

6. Set the prefix back to the CONFIG folder:

    ```
    PFX 2/CONFIG
    ```

7. Load and Assemble:

    ```
    CONFIG/
              CONFIG
              INITSTR
    ```

8. In the editor, type Command-O to get the "Command:" prompt box.

9. Type "link make" and press Return. The resulting file is:

    ```
    CONFIG.SYSTEM
    ```

10. Switch to the ACOS folder:

```
PFX 2/ACOS
```

11. Load and Assemble:

```
ACOS/
        ACOS
        ACOS.LOAD
```

Resulting files are:

```
        ACOS.OBJ
        ENCODE
        ACOS.SYSTEM
```

12. Now, copy ACOS.OBJ, ENCODE and ACOS from the Acos folder to your master GBBS.CONFIG folder. Then copy CONFIG.SYSTEM from the Config folder to your master GBBS. CONFIG folder.

Your master **GBBS.CONFIG** folder should contain:

```
        PRODOS
        ACOS
        ACOS.OBJ
        CONFIG.SYSTEM
        ENCODE
        BC.S
        LOGON.SEG.S
        MAIN.SEG.S
        MSG.CONVERT.S
        MSG.SEG.S
        NEW.MSG.FIX.S
        SYSTEM.SEG.S
        USER.CONVERT.S
```

Your master **GBBS.SYSTEM** folder should contain:

```
B1
BBS
DATA
DATA1
DATA2
D1
D1.1
D1.2
D1.3
D1.4
G1
G1.1
G1.2
HLP.EDIT
HLP.MAIN
HLP.MSG
HLP.USER
HLP.XFER
MAIL
MNU.NEW
MNU.VAL.40
NMU.VAL.80
SYS.INFO
SYS.NEWINFO
SYS.NEWS
SYS.QUESTIONS
USERS
V1.1
V1.2
V1.3
V1.4
X.DN
X.UP
XDOS
```

*** INSTALLED FOLDERS ***

Where 'v' is the base path, usually the volume name:

```
A: v/GBBS.PRO/PROGRAM
B: v/GBBS.PRO/SYSTEM
C: v/GBBS.PRO/GFILES
D: v/GBBS.PRO/DOWNLOAD
E: v/GBBS.PRO/UPLOAD
F: v/GBBS.PRO/BULLETINS
G: v/GBBS.PRO/MAIL
```

*** MEMORY ***

```
$800  - CONFIG
$900  - CONSOLE DRIVER
$C00  - PRINTER DRIVER
$D00  - CLOCK DRIVER
$E00  - MODEM DRIVER
$1200 - ENTRY POINT (START)
        JSR   MDMINIT
        JSR   VIDINIT
```

*** OLD FILES ***

It is assumed that only the files that are used are now in the main folders above. In each may or may not be an "old" folder that contains files that did not seem to be used, or were old or otherwise modified versions of files. We tried to pick the latest, but it was not always clear which those were.

ACOS/OLD

    ACOSLOAD.ASM
    ACOS.LOAD1
    ACOSA
    ATLK.TEST
    ACOS.LOAD.OLD
    INITA
    CMD2A

CONFIG/CLOCKS/OLD

    HEADER   (unused?)
    CLK.IIC.SYS   (partial implementation?)
    NSC2X   (ACOS No Slot Clock)

CONFIG/MODEMS/OLD

    ACOS.GS.DVR   (unused?)
    GSPORT.HST2   (PRE DTE)
    GSPORT.NEW1   (1991 16K Buffers
    GSPORT.NEW2   by Andy Nicholas)
    GSPORT.SLOT1   (original)
    GSPORT.SLOT2   (original)
    HAYES.NEW2   (rel/GSPORT version)
    HAYES.ULTRA   (1991 16K Buffers by Andy Nicholas)
    HAYES.ULTRA1   (original)
    HAYES.ULTRA2   (original)
    SSC.INT   (USRobotics with Commented out code)
    SSC.INTERRUPT   (USRobotics)

CONFIG/PRINTERS/OLD

    PRINTERS   (combines all drivers into a single file,
                       "printers")

Glossary

This glossary contains some of the common terms that are used in this manual, and some terms that you may read or hear when working with data communications. The terms are described only as they relate to data communications and the ACOS language, and not necessarily with the full definition.

1,200 BPS – One of the most common speeds used for data communications over dial-up telephone lines, equal to approximately 120 characters per second (cps).

2,400 BPS – The fastest of the widely-used speeds for connections between PC's and mainframes over dial-up telephone lines, equal to approximately 240 characters per second (cps).

300 BPS – A common standard transmission speed for fast mechanical terminals and for video terminals communicating over telephone lines.

6502 / 65C02 – The microprocessor at the heart of your Apple II.

9,600 BPS – The fastest common transmission speed available on many terminals and other peripheral devices and over ordinary telephone lines.

38,400 BPS – The fastest transmission speed available with *GBBS Pro* and the Apple Super Serial Card.

ACCESS – To send or receive data from a bulletin board to a user calling the system.

ACKNOWLEDGEMENT CHARACTER (ACK) – In binary synchronous communications, a transmission control character sent as positive response to a data transmission.

ACOS – An acronym for All-purpose Communications Operating System. This is a powerful language, developed by Greg Schaefer, tailored to communications applications.

ALGORITHM – A sequence of steps which may be performed by a program or other process, which will produce a given result.

ALPHABETIC CHARACTER – Any one of the letters A through Z (uppercase and lowercase).

ALPHANUMERIC – Consisting of letters, numbers, and other symbols such as punctuation marks and mathematical symbols.

ANALOG SIGNALS – Continuously variable data signals, such as voice signals or a sine wave. A modem will convert digital data into analog signals in order to transmit data over a phone line. The receiving modem converts the analog signals back to digital data.

APPLE – (1) The round fleshy fruit of a Rosaceous tree (Pyrus Malus). (2) A brand of personal computer. (3) Apple Computer, Inc. manufacturer of home computers.

ARGUMENT – The value on which a function operates.

ARITHMETIC OPERATOR – An operator, such as +, that combines numeric values to produce a numeric result.

ARRAY – A set of data or other items in a structured pattern.

ASCII (American Standard Code for Information Interchange) – This is a character encoding standard that translates uppercase and lowercase letters and symbolic characters into a 7-bit binary representation having the values 0 to 127. The eighth bit, parity and framing bits are not part of this definition.

ASSEMBLER – A program used to translate as assembly language program into the machine language used by a processor.

ASSEMBLY LANGUAGE – A language similar in structure to machine language, but made up of "mnemonics" and "symbols" that are converted to the machine language of a processor by the assembler.

ASYNCHRONOUS COMMUNICATION – A method of transferring data one-bit-at-a-time, with start and stop bits separating each byte of data during a specific time interval. However, the start of each character or block of characters can occur at any time during this interval. Contrast with "Synchronous Transmission."

AUTO-ANSWER, AUTO-DIAL, AUTO-REDIAL – This allows the modem to send and receive data unattended. The auto-redial feature allows modems to redial a busy line or try to re-establish an unintentionally broken connection.

BACKUP – A process in which the user makes a duplicate copy of programs and files that can be used in the event of a malfunction or loss of the original data. After the *GBBS* system is configured, a backup should be made of system files. A weekly backup should be made of every data file on the system including the data file, user file, bulletin boards, and the mail file.

BASIC (Beginner's All-purpose Symbolic Instruction Code) – A programming language designed for interactive systems and originally developed at Dartmouth College to encourage people to use computers for simple problem-solving operations.

BAUD – The number of changes in signal levels, frequency, or phase per second on a communication channel. If each represents one bit of data, baud is the same as bits per second. However, it is possible for one signal change (one baud) to equal more than one bit of data.

BBS (Bulletin Board System) – A computer that allows users to dial into the system over a phone line or telnet connection, log in, and leave messages in different topic groups. Users can read and reply to public messages, send private email to users of that BBS, share files, and play games. BBSs were at their peak in the 1980s with commercial services like CompuServe and GEnie, as well as thousands of systems run by hobbyists.

BELL COMPATIBILITY – Modems made to conform to design and transmission standards developed by AT&T, which invented the modem. AT&T established the Bell 103, 113, and 212A standards for designing modems that transmit at various speeds.

BINARY – Pertaining to a system of numbers to the base two, the binary digits are 0 and 1.

BINARY SYNCHRONOUS COMMUNICATIONS (BSC) (BISYNC) – A form of communications line control that uses transmission control characters to control the transfer of data over a communications line.

BIT – Abbreviation for "Binary DigIT." Either of the binary digits 0 or 1. See *Byte*.

BITS PER SECOND (BPS) – A measure of data-transmission speed, equal to the number of signal changes per second.

BLOAD – Binary program load.

BRUN – Binary program run. The BRUN command in DOS 3.3 and ProDOS causes a binary program to be loaded into memory and run.

BSAVE – Binary program save. The BSAVE command in DOS 3.3 and ProDOS causes the binary data in some portion of memory to be saved as a disk file.

BOOT – The process of starting a computer system ("booting up"). A cold boot is starting the computer after it was off. The operating system (DOS 3.3 or ProDOS) is loaded into memory. A warm boot is a reloading of the operating system without a power-down sequence.

BRANCH – An instruction which causes program execution to jump to a new point in the program sequence rather than execute the next instruction in the program.

BREAK – A signal that says that the normal flow of data should be interrupted on the data line for approximately 300 milliseconds.

BREAKOUT BOX – A test device used for monitoring and inserting signals at the RS-232 level.

BUFFER – (1) A temporary storage unit, especially one that accepts information at one rate and delivers it at another rate. (2) An area of storage, temporarily reserved for performing input or output, into which data is read from which data is written.

BUG – An undocumented feature.

BYTE – The amount of storage required to represent one character. Hexadecimal or Decimal representation of eight binary bits: 0~255 in Decimal, $00~$FF in Hexidecimal. 8 bits = 1 byte. 1,024 bytes = 1K or Kilobyte.

CALL FORWARDING – Calls to one station can be automatically switched to another specified station.

CALL WAITING – A second call to one station at the same time the station has a call, will interrupt the station to let them know they have a second call. If the first call is with a modem, then the modem's carrier will be interrupted and disconnected. Call Forwarding is recommended to solve this problem.

CARRIAGE RETURN – The key that is used as an end of line or end or input terminator. Also called the RETURN key.

CARRIER – An analog signal that is a continuous frequency that can be modulated with a second (information-carrying) signal.

CATALOG – A list of all files stored on a disk, sometimes called a "directory."

CCITT COMPATIBILITY – Conforms to international standards for data transmissions established by the Comitte' Consultatif International Telephonique and Telepraphique. The French version of *GBBS II* supports this standard.

CHARACTER – A letter, digit, or other symbol.

CHAT – This command allows two computers to communicate with typed messages that are displayed on both monitors at the same time.

CHECKSUM – A value calculated on the total number of bytes in a block of data. This is used for error detection and correction when transferring files using the Xmodem protocol.

CHRISTENSEN PROTOCOL – A very common error-free protocol developed in the late 1970s by Ward Christensen.

CLOCK – A circuit which provides synchronizing signals for the various components of a computer system.

CODE – (1) A number or symbol used to represent some piece of information in a compact or easily processed form. (2) The statements or instructions that make up a program.

COMPILER – A program which translates a high-level language into the machine code used by a computer.

CONDITIONAL BRANCH – A branch that depends on the truth of a condition or the value of an expression.

CONDITIONING – A technique of applying electronic filtering elements to a communications line to improve the capability of that line to support higher transmission rates of data on that line.

CONFIGURATION: CONFIG – A process that specifies the type of computer, video display, modem and interface card to add the proper drivers to the *GBBS Pro* system.

CONSOLE – The part of the computer used for communications between the operator and the computer.

CONSTANT – A symbol in a program representing a fixed, unchanging value. Compare to "Variable."

CONTROL CHARACTER – A special character created by simultaneously typing the control key and another alpha character. These keys are used in the editor for cursor movement and text formatting. Control characters are shown as their alphanumeric equivalent preceded by a carat "^". Control-G is shown as ^G.

CURSOR – (1) A marker or symbol that delineates where the next action will take place. (2) A Sysop who is adding new mods which kill his data file.

CYCLIC REDUNDANCY CHECK (CRC) – A mathematical progression involving the binary value of data bytes used for error sensing and correction when transferring files in protocol mode.

DASH (-) – This command runs a BASIC, machine, EXEC, or interpreter program in ProDOS only.

DATA BITS – The number of bits used for sending each character, not including the added checking and timing bits.

DATA COMPRESSION – A feature of *GBBS Pro* to pack 7 bits of data into 8 bits, resulting in a 30% increase of data storage.

DEBUGGING – The process of detecting and correcting errors in a computer program.

DEFAULT – The value used if a RETURN is entered in response to a request for specific data in place of the user typing in the information.

DELETE – The command that removes a file from its directory.

DELIMITER – A character that is used for punctuation to mark the beginning or end of a sequence of characters, and is not considered part of the sequence itself. ACOS uses the double quotation mark (") for PRINT statements.

DIGITAL DATA – Data represented by on and off conditions called bits, used for the transfer of binary data.

DISCONNECT – The termination of the connection between a user and the *GBBS Pro* system.

DIRECTORY – A list of files on your diskette or part of a group of files on a hard drive. In ProDOS, each directory has a name rather that the "Slot x, Drive x, Volume x" designation in DOS 3.3.

DISK OPERATING SYSTEM (DOS) – The user interface between computer and the applications program. An operating system allows the user to execute programs and perform disk operations. The Sysop has access to the important DOS commands in *GBBS Pro* in the system segment.

DISTORTION – An undesirable change in a data communications signal.

DOWNLOAD – To send a file from your *GBBS* system to a user, usually in the Transfer section of your Bulletin Board. Downloading requires some way to synchronize the sending of the file by one system with the receiving and storing of the data by the other. Both ASCII and XMODEM downloading is offered by *GBBS Pro*.

DTR / Data Terminal Ready – On the RS-232 connection, the DTR line is used to tell the modem that the computer is ready for operation.

DUPLEX – Pertains to communications in the way data is sent between computers. Full Duplex characters sent to a host computer will be echoed back to the caller's screen. In Half Duplex, the caller's software is responsible for displaying characters typed while talking to a host computer on the local screen. The host computer only sends responses out in one direction.

EDITOR – A text-editing program that allows text to be entered into a data file and manipulated as desired.

EMULATION – The act of imitating another computer's video display characteristics.

ENQ (Enquire) – The transmission control character, Control-E, usually used to request a response from the remote system.

ERROR MESSAGE – A message ACOS displays to notify the user of an error or problem in the execution of the program.

ESC (Escape) – The control character, Control-[, to cancel or abort a function.

EXEC – This command causes input to be taken from a sequential text file rather than from the keyboard.

EXECUTE – To perform an action specified by a program or computer operator.

EXPRESSION – A formula in a program describing a calculation to be performed.

FIRMWARE – Those components of a computer system consisting of programs stored permanently in read-only memory. Printer cards have firmware in them.

FLAG – A data bit used to indicate the state of a device or the result of an operation.

FLOW CONTROL – The method of controlling the flow of data by starting and stopping what one computer is sending/receiving to another. The receiver sends an XOFF character to stop the sender, and an XON character to restart it.

FORMAT – To prepare a blank diskette to receive information by dividing its surface into tracks and sectors.

FREEWARE – Software that is distributed to people freely, but a donation to the author is required when used. Check with the author before posting Freeware on your board.

FREQUENCY MODULATION – Modifying the frequency of a carrier signal so it can carry data signals.

GATEWAY – A connection between two dissimilar networks.

GBBS II – The original Bulletin Board System by Greg Schaefer written in BASIC with machine language drivers.

HANDSHAKE – The exchange or detection of certain characters to establish synchronization for a data path.

HEXADECIMAL – The base 16 number system, composed of the numbers 0 through 9, and A through F. Usually notated with a '$' prefix. Hexadecimal is a useful shorthand for describing the contents of a byte, with each hex digit describing half of a byte.

HOST – In this case, the host is the *GBBS Pro* system that answers the incoming call and establishes the Answer carrier tone. It is the primary regulator of the data exchange. The calling computer is the originator using an originate carrier tone.

INITIALIZE – (1) To set to an initial state or value in preparation for some computation. (2) To prepare a blank disk to receive information by dividing its surface into tracks and sectors.

INPUT – (1) Information transferred into a computer from some external source, such as the keyboard, a disk drive, or a modem. (2) The act or process of transferring such information.

INTERFACE – A device that links two parts together and converts signals of one type to those of another type.

INTERPRETER – A program which translates instructions written in a high level to machine code as the program is executed.

INTERRUPT – (1) To temporarily stop a process. (2) In data communications, to take an action at a receiving computer that causes the ending computer to end a transmission.

I/O (Input/Output) – The transfer of information in and out of a computer.

JOYSTICK – A lever that can pivot in all directions and that is used as a locator device.

JUMP – Essentially another term for a branch.

K (Kilobyte) – Used with numbers to denote "kilo" or one thousand. 1K = 1024 bytes.

KERMIT – An error-free protocol generally used for text transfers, developed by Columbia University.

LINEFEED – Moves the cursor on the screen down one line. The ASCII character is Control-J.

LINKER – A program used to link together blocks of assembly language or ACOS code to form an executable program.

LOCAL – When referring to a BBS, the local means access via a keyboard that is connected to the computer by wire, rather than via a remote communications link or modem connection.

LOAD – This command brings a BASIC program into memory from a file.

LOADER – A program which calls up machine code from mass storage and loads it into memory for execution.

LOCK – This commands protects a file from being accidentally renamed, deleted, or altered.

LOG – (1) The act of changing to another drive, user area or directory path in a program or operating system. (2) The record kept in a file called "LOG" of each user that calls *GBBS Pro*.

LOG IN / LOG ON – The act of connecting to *GBS Pro* bulletin board using the user number and password. A new user will go through the login sequence to become verified.

LOG OUT / LOG OFF – The act of disconnecting from *GBBS Pro* bulletin board when a user is finished accessing the system.

LOGICAL OPERATOR – An operator, such as AND, that combines logical values to produce a logical result.

LOOP – A section of a program that is executed repeatedly until some condition is met such as an index variable reaching a specified ending value.

M – Mega or million.

MACHINE LANGUAGE – Data groups which are interpreted as instructions to be executed by the processor.

MACRO – The use of single keys or short sequences of keys to recall stored user number, password and other phrases to log onto *GBBS Pro* and use different parts of the system.

MEMORY LOCATION – A unit of main memory that is identified by an address and can hold a single item of information of a fixed size. In the Apple II, a memory location holds one byte, or 8 bits of information.

MENU – A list of options presented by a program.

MICROPROCESSOR – A computer processor contained in a single integrated circuit, such as the Apple II's 6502 microprocessor.

MNP – An error free, full-duplex protocol implemented at the modem firmware level. It does automatic error checking that is transparent to the applications running such as ACOS.

MODE – A state of a computer or system that determines its behavior.

MODEM – A contraction of MODulator/DEModulator. It is a device used for converting digital signals into analog signals and vice versa, that allows computers to communicate directly with each other.

MONITOR – (1) A closed-circuit television receiver. (2) A program which allows you to use your computer at a very low level, often with the values and addresses of individual memory locations.

NEGATIVE ACKNOWLEDGEMENT CHARACTER (NAK) – In binary synchronous communications, a transmission of Control-U sent as a negative response to data received.

NETWORK – A collections of data processing products connected by communications lines for information exchange between computers or mail systems.

NIBBLE (or Nybble) – (1) A 4-bit unit of data, or half a byte. (2) One of the best and longest-running magazines for the Apple II and Mac, created by entrepreneur and business expert Mike Harvey. (3) "What are we going to call this series of bits? How about a bite, but spell it with a 'y'! So what do we call half a byte? A 'nybble', obviously!" (attributed to Werner Buchholz at IBM, circa 1956.)

NOISE / LINE NOISE – Undesirable electrical signals on the communications channel that can interfere or distort data signals.

NULL – The null character CONTROL-@ used for producing a delay after carriage return linefeed sequences by *GBBS Pro*.

NULL MODEM – (1) A device that allows two DTE devices to be connected together without using a modem. (2) To install a Null Modem as the modem, *GBBS Pro* will allow you to run the program with no modem attached.

OBJECT PROGRAM – The program produced by a compiler or interpreter from a high-level program.

OFF-LINE – The state in which the computer is not connected to another computer and the modem is inactive.

ON-LINE – The state in which the computer is connected to another computer and the modem is active.

OPEN – This command allocates space in memory for a files buffers, and sets the file position pointer to the beginning of the file.

OPERATOR – A symbol or sequence of characters such as + or AND, specifying an operation to be performed on one or more values (the operands) to produce a result.

OUTPUT – (1) Information transferred from a computer to some external destination, such as the display screen, a disk drive, a printer, or a modem. (2) The act or process of transferring such information.

PARALLEL – A method of data handling in which all the bits composing a word are transmitted simultaneously.

PARAMETER – A value supplied to a program that either is used as input, or controls the actions of the program.

PARITY – The method of setting or clearing a final data bit by adding the valid data bits of a byte to form and even or odd value for error detection. Parity may turned off, (NONE) set for a constant 1 or 0 bit ("mark" and "space" respectively).

PATH – A specified route to a specific subdirectory used in ProDOS.

PERIPHERAL – An external device connected to a computer such as a printer, a modem, a monitor, or a disk drive.

PHASE MODULATION – Altering the phase of a carrier signal to convey data signals.

POINTER – A register memory location containing the memory address of data or instructions.

POLLING – A method for determining whether the other computer has data to send.

PR# – This command sends output to the Apple II slot number specified.

PREFIX – A settable pathname that indicates a directory file.

PROCESSOR – A generic term for that part of computer hardware performing arithmetic and logical operations.

ProDOS – This major operating system of Apple II computers, that stands for Professional Disk Operating System.

PROGRAM – A sequence of instructions to be followed by the computer to carry out desired operations.

PROMPT – To remind or signal the user that some action is expected, typically by displaying a distinctive symbol, a reminder message, or a menu of choices on the display screen.

PROTOCOL – A set of rules for exchange of data between computers. Handshaking, error detection and correction methods may be used.

PUBLIC DOMAIN – Software that is not copyrighted and may be distributed freely.

QUIT – Exiting a program and returning to the operating system.

RAM (Random Access Memory) – The volatile, temporary storage area in the computer, accessible until it is turned off.

RAM DRIVE – The use of RAM to emulate a disk drive for temporary drive storage.

READ – To transfer information into the computers memory from a source external to the computer (such as a disk drive or modem), or into the computers processor from a source external to the processor (such as a keyboard or main memory).

RELATIONAL OPERATOR – An operator, such as >, that compares numeric values to produce a logical result.

REMOTE – When referring to a BBS, the remote is the user who is connected to the computer via a communications link and modem rather than directly by wire.

REMOTE DIGITAL LOOP-BACK – A modem can either test another device's ability to process digital signals (remote loop-back) or it can test its own ability to process signals (local loop-back).

RENAME – Change the name of the file.

RESERVED WORD – A word or sequence of characters reserved by ACOS for some specific use, and therefore unavailable as a variable name in a program.

RESET – A key, which is part of a combination that causes the computer to re-boot a program.

ROM (Read Only Memory) – A memory device from which data can be read, but the data cannot be altered or added to.

RS-232 – A standard voltage interface allowing a serial connection between the computer's communications port and an external device such as a modem or a printer.

RUN – To execute a BASIC program.

RUN-TIME – The actual execution time of when a program is started.

SAVE – This command lets you save the BASIC program currently in memory to a file on disk.

SEGMENT – A section of a larger program. Within itself, a segment is a small program of its own which is usually linked to other segments under ACOS.

SELF TEST – Most modems have the ability to test their circuits to ensure they are in working order, before being setup to send and receive signals.

SERIAL – A method of data handling in which the bits composing a word are transmitted one after the other.

SMART MODEM – Usually an ASCII-controlled intelligent modem. Provides special dialing features and the ability to auto-answer an incoming phone call under manual or software control.

STACK – A series of registers or memory used to hold an address or data.

START BIT – Since there is no signal sent to keep timing if there is a gap between characters, a timing bit used to indicate the start of a new character during serial asynchronous transmission.

STATEMENT – An instruction line in a high-level language.

STOP BIT – An extra bit (or bits) is added after each character to tell the receiving system that the character has ended and the following bit stream will be part of the next character.

STRING – A group of ASCII characters that are alpha, numeric, punctuation, or control.

SUBROUTINE – A section of frequently used operations in a program which are treated as small separate programs.

SYNCHRONOUS COMMUNICATION – Communications between computers and modems that can send and receive on precise synchronization.

SYNTAX – The formal structure of an argument or command.

SYSOP – System Operator of a BBS. Pronounced "Sis-op."

TIME OUT – An indication that the computer communicating with your *GBBS* system has been inactive for a specified length of time, and is disconnected and logged off by your system.

TOGGLE – Switching between one of two states of conditions (e.g. On or Off, Up or Down, Half or Full).

TRACE – A debugging method in which the program is executed one instruction at a time, and sometimes the register contents can be examined after each step.

TRANSPOSE – The reversal of the roles of a destructive backspace and non-destructive backspace in the User configuration for the editor.

TTY – An abbreviation for Teletype.

UPLOAD – The process of sending a file from the user's system to *GBBS Pro*. Uploading requires some way to synchronize the sending of the file from the user's system with the receiving and storing of data by the Bulletin Board. Both ASCII and XMODEM uploading is offered by *GBBS Pro*.

USER FRIENDLY – A term used to describe hardware and software which does not require extensive computer knowledge or experience to successfully use. Another term to describe *GBBS Pro*.

VARIABLE – (1) A location in the computer's memory where a value can be stored. (2) The symbol used in a program to represent such a location.

VOLUME – Under an operating system, a volume is a unit of storage.

WORD – One or more contiguous bytes.

WORDWRAP – The automatic continuation of text from the end of one line to the beginning of the next, as on the display screen or a printer.

WOZ – Steve Wozniak, an Apple Computer Inc. co-founder, inventor of the Apple-1 and Apple II computers, all-around genius, nice guy, über geek, philanthropist, and a legal string assignment in *GBBS*.

WRITE – To transfer information from the computer to a destination external to the computer (such as a disk drive or modem) or from the computers processor (such as main memory).

XOFF – An ASCII character (Control-S) used for pausing data transmission between *GBBS Pro* and the user in either direction.

XON – An ASCII character (Control-Q) used to restart the data transmission is suspended by an XOFF. Other characters are also supported by *GBBS Pro*.

X.25 – A specification of the CCITT that defines the connection of data terminal equipment to an X.25 network.

X.PC – A full-duplex, error-free protocol designed for micro-computers to transfer files. This protocol was developed by Tymnet and is based on the CCITT X.25 network protocol.

XMODEM – A name used to describe the primary transfer protocol. The protocol transfers data in 128 byte blocks and uses a checksum to check for any errors in the transfer.

YMODEM – A faster and more reliable transfer protocol created to accompany *GBBS* through additional plugins. Originally developed on CPM for batch file transfers using 1K blocks, Ward Christensen called it YMODEM in his implementation of the protocol.

Y – (1) Questions that sysops ask that have no answer. (2) A glossary entry to help complete the alphabet.

ZMODEM – The most reliable and useful transfer protocol, also available to accompany *GBBS* through additional plugins. The ZMODEM protocol allows for transfers to be interrupted and resumed at a later time without having to re-transfer the first part of the data.

ZULU TIME – A common term for 24-hour time based on Greenwich Mean Time (GMT). It is often used in computer-connection networks spanning large areas and several time zones.

```
[11:02] [MAIN LEVEL] (?=Help):BYE

Terminate Connection


Are you sure? (Y/[N]):Y


Goodbye Woz,

You were caller #1976
Connected 65 min, 02 sec

Thank you for calling The A.P.P.L.E. Crate BBS


          Live Long and Prosper...
```